THE VALMIKI RAMAYAN

PART-I

KONDA MURALI

Copyright © Konda Murali
All Rights Reserved.

To mother and father, it is impossible to thank you adequately for everthing you have done, from loving me unconditionally to raising me in a stable household, where you instilled morals and traditional values in me.

Konda Murali

Author and Poet

9441431090

Contents

Foreword

I feel very happy to read The Valmiki Ramayan in English version, wriiten by Konda Murali. The author's effort to make known the Indian culture to the present generation. He is trying to make them aware of Indian epics The Ramayan and The Mahabharath so that they would learn many life skiills. I read some of Konda Murali's books. After reading them, I wouldn't be without appreciating his deep insight into the human nature and the society. I hope this book would impact on the readers lot.

Sabitha Indra Reddy
Education Minister, Telangana

Preface

Konda Murali is a reputed author and poet of 16 best selling books. He writes anthologies, novels and academic books. He is a government teacher in Telangana Gurukula Schools. He hails from Hyderabad, Telangana.

Acknowledgements

I wish to express my deep gratitude and thanks to my family and friends. Their encouragement keeps me motivating to be in writing field. With their suppport, I could complete 16 books. So I take this opportunity to express my deep sense of gratitude to them.

Prologue

The basic teaching of Ramayana is that no matter how powerful evil is, it will always be defeated by Good. Truth always wins, no matter how vicious or poisonous lie is because even a bitter truth oozes with positivity and the sweetest lie has the darkest agenda behind it. The win of good over evil is a universal fate.

Ayodhya Kanda is one of the important kandas in Ramayan and narrates the arrangements for Lord Rama's coronation and his exile into the wilderness for a period of fourteen years in order to fulfil his father's wish. The kanda portrays the obedience and determination of Rama who refused to return to Ayodhya without fulfilling his father'orders. It involves the exchange between King Dashratha and his queen Kaikeyi, where the latter asks for her two boons. The kand throws light on the calm self-control character of Rama who with absolute submission accepted his father's decree for the sake of his honour. It also shows the sacrifice of Sita and Laxmana who decided to stay with Rama during the exile.

The book discusses the episodes of Aranyakanda and Kishkindakanda in the Ramayan. It depicted how Ravana abducted Sita for Laxmana hurting his sister, Surpanaka and for Rama killing fourteen thousands of his soldiers. And how Rama with anxiousness started searching for Sita.

CHAPTER ONE

Balakanda

There was a country called Kosala on the bank of the sacred river, Sarayu. It was a country which flourished with abundant treasure. The capital city of Kosala was Ayodhya which was technically constructed with human wisdom. The streets of the city were wide and broad, and looked awesome in those days. In this sacred city, there was a king who lived and ruled the country significantly. His name was King Dasharatha. This king used to rule his country and his people as if his own sons and daughters.

The people in this city were righteous and honest. They were very rich but no vanity. The people were praised all over the world because of their wisdom and their humbleness. The king's ministers were also very sophisticated and had a lot of common sense. And they always used to think about the people's welfare. Vashishtha and Vamadeva were their teachers. To our surprise, there were no cruel people in that kingdom. That was the greatness of the kingdom.

There were no Kings as great as Dasaratha in those days. His kingdom is even to be compared with the lord Indra so his Kingdom was treated as heaven. The king was very sacred and with a lot of wisdom but he did not have offspring. So that made him very sad. The great Saints in his

Kingdom suggested that he go to Ashwamedha Yagya. So he ordered his ministers Sumantra to take the saints, rishis and priests to do Ashwamedha Yagna.

So the Minister obeyed the order of King Dasaratha and brought the most famous priests who were very knowledgeable at Vedas. Their names were Suyagna, Vamadeva and Jabali. And he also brought some other priests to be helpful to them to the kingdom.

Then the king Dasaratha explained to the priests his problem and told them he wanted to perform Ashwamedha Yagya for the offspring. He told them without sons or daughters his life would be vain. On hearing the words of the King Dasaratha, the priests felt very happy and appreciated him for having the dream to perform Ashwamedha Yagya. With a lot of enthusiasm, they told the king to get them the commodities which were needed for the Yagna. They told him to let loose the horse before they do Yagna. Since the yagna was being performed on the bank of the Sarayu river, he would definitely be blessed with offspring.

On hearing the words of the priests, the king was very happy. He ordered his soldiers to let loose the horse and told them to celebrate themselves on the occasion of the yagna. Later they decided to perform the yagna on the north side of the river Sarayu then only it will be performed without any fault. The king also told the people to be supportive until the yagna completes. Everybody obeyed the orders of the king and went to their homes.

Sumantra spoke to the king, Dasharatha privately that he would be blessed with sons with the blessings of Rishyasrunga who was the grandson of Sanathkamara. He also told the king, "Once there was a hermit named

Kashyapa Maharshi. He had a son named Rishyasringa. Rishyasringa grew up in the forest used to roam in it. He never disobeyed the orders of his father. He was a very humble son. Since he was a Brahmin, he used to live with two principles. One was to live as a bachelor having fire as his food and the other was to follow his father's instructions. His lifestyle was adored by the people in those days. Kashyapa Maharshi used to have the fire as his food. Then Romapada was their king. He was a very powerful king but unfortunately the dreadful drought occurred. The drought terrified the people with the lack of rain. The king felt unhappy with the people's pathetic conditions. To do something as preventive measurements, the king called the priests. He told them to do something. Then the priests replied to the king to call Rishyasringa. He was adept at the Vedas. So if the king marries his daughter, Shantha to Rishyasrunga, the kingdom flourishes with the rains and crops. And the problems of the people would be solved. On hearing the words of the priests, he told his soldiers to bring Rishyasringa to the kingdom. But the soldiers were afraid of the hermit and told the king they would not go to bring him. So the king sent prostitutes to bring him. As soon as he stepped in the kingdom, it rained heavily and people felt very happy. Later the king did the marriage his daughter with Rishyasrunga"

The king, Dasharatha asked Sumantra how Romapada could easily bring Rishyasringa to the kingdom. Then Sumantra told him that he had used the prostitutes as bait to him. The prostitutes decorated themselves beautifully to attract him. Rishyasrunga was wandering in the forest, when they went. They were distracted with their performances and brought him to the kingdom. The king was interestingly listening to Sumantra who was resuming.

He told the king that for some days Rishyasrunga did not come out of his Ashram as he was a man of austerity. He did not know the difference between the male and female. But one day he came out of the ashram and saw the prostitutes and wondered with their physical appearance. The prostitutes asked what he was doing alone in the forest. Rishyasrunga who had not seen such prostitutes before, astonished looking at them. He said that he was the son of Vibandaka Maharshi. Their ashram was near to the place. When the prostitutes asked him to teach Brahma Gnana, he told them to come to his ashram. There he would reveal the gnana.

The prostitutes went to his place. He gave them fruits, roots and stems. The prostitutes had them.

On seeing Vibandaka Maharshi, they were afraid of him and they fled from the place. Rishyasrunga became dull after the prostitutes had gone.

The next day he started searching for the prostitutes and found somewhere in the forest. On seeing them, he felt very happy. The prostitutes asked to come to their ashram and there they would give him the strange stems. The prostitutes used enchanted words to attract him. With the words he felt very happy. Since he lost his senses, he promised to come along with them. Later the prostitutes took him to the kingdom. The king, Romapada, was very careful about Vibandaka Maharshi. So the king satisfied him. Later the king took Rishyasrunga into the palace and did the marriage with his daughter, Shantha.

Rishyasrunga thus started living in the palace with his wife.

Sumatra went to the kingdom of Romapada to bring

Rishyasringa. He told everything about the king, Dasaratha. On hearing about Ashwamedha Yagna, Romapada felt very happy and sent Rishyasrunga along with Shantha to Ayodhya to perform Ashwamedha Yagna. On seeing Rishyasringa, the king Dasaratha felt very happy.

After some days, the king, Dasharatha decided to perform Ashwamedha Yagna as spring season arrived. He asked Rishyasrunga to perform the yagna for the offspring. The son of hermit asked to provide the necessities to perform it, let loose the horse and to show the land where the yagna was to be performed. The king invited the priests who were good at the Vedas. The priests came and praised the king for his desire of performing the yagna.

The king took the blessings of Vashishta Maharshi and he blessed the king that the yagna would resume without any disturbances. Vashishta Maharshi ordered the carpenters, priests, merchants and labourers to contribute their part and give encouragement to the yagna. All the people of Ayodhya prepared and decorated the place for the yagna. Vashishta told the king to observe the place where the yagna would be performed.

As per the instruction of Vashishta, the king, Dasharatha went to the place one auspicious day. After the king had gone to the place, Vashishta accompanied Rishyasrunga and the other priests to the place. Later they started Ashwametha Yagna. The king and his three wives were fasting. A year later, the horse came back to the place. Later Ashwametha Yagna was started by Rishyasrunga and the other priests. They invited the gods with their melodious chants and songs. They prayed and provided the consumables to the gods.

There were no people in the country with hunger and with sadness while the yagna was being performed.

Delicious food, new clothes were provided to the men and women in the kingdom. Twenty one poles were decorated with flowers and colourful clothes. The king gave the east part to Hotha, west part to Adharvu, south part to Brahma and north part to Udghatha as the yagna's honorarium. Later Rishyasrunga blessed him that he would get four sons as the result of the yagna. On hearing that, the king felt very happy.

Then Rishyasrunga told the king that he even had to perform other yagna with sacred chanting. While it was being performed all the gods gathered at the yagna and prayed to Vishnu that he would have to kill Ravana. The god Vishnu promised the gods that they would kill Ravana in the war. Later Vishnu himself chose Dasharatha as his father. After the yagna had been completed, Rishyasrunga gave a divine dessert to the king which was in the golden pot. He told him that the divine dessert was given by the gods and suggested that he make it by his three wives.

The king came to his palace with the golden pot. When he came to the palace, it shone brightly. He went to his first wife, Kausalya and told her to have it. Kausalya drank half of the pot. Later he gave it second wife, Sumitra and she drank half of it. The rest was given to the third wife, Kaikeyi but she drank only half of it and gave it back to Sumitra. The remaining dessert was drunk by Sumitra again.

After the three wives had had the dessert, they were conceived. On hearing the news even the gods felt very happy because the lord, Vishnu himself became the son of the king, Dasharatha. The gods requested lord Brahma to make other sons of Dasharatha who were intelligent, brave. So they would be equal to the lord, Vishnu.

After Ashwametha Yagna was performed, the gods took their parts and went to heaven. The kings, who attended the yagna, went back to their kingdoms, appreciating Dasharatha for performing the yagna in a very good manner. Even Rishyasrunga went back with his wife, Shantha to his ashram. After everyone had gone, Dasharatha waited for twelve months for the sons' birth. After a year on Chaitra Navami when five planets were in the same line, on cancer zodiac lagna in Punarvasu star, the lord, Vishnu himself was born as Srirama from the womb of Kausalya. Srirama was shining as if he was the lord, Indra. The fourth part of the lord, Vishnu was born as Bharatha to Kaikeyi. Later Sumitra gave birth to Laxmana and Shathrugna. During their births, Gandharvas sang melodious songs. Nature thrilled and it drizzled with flowers rain. The people of Ayodhya celebrated the festival by decorating their houses and the streets. Dasharatha donated money and gold to the people and to the priests.

On the eleventh day, the Cradle Ceremony was held. The first child was named as Srirama, second as Bharatha, third as Laxmana and the fourth as Shathrugna. Of all the children, Srirama had become dear to Dasharatha and to the people of Ayodhya. The four children were taught Vedas and archery even from their childhood. They could become very good warriors. Of all, Srirama could become a very good warrior. He could learn to ride horses, elephants and chariots. He had shown very much interest in Dhanurveda.

Srirama and Laxmana had become very close friends. Laxmana used to accompany Srirama wherever they went. They used to eat and sleep together. They even used to go hunting together. Dasharatha's misery had become happiness because of his four sons. He felt very happy with his sons. Like Srirama and Laxmana. Bharatha and Shathrugna were good friends. The four children were prodigies and with very good human qualities. Since everything was good about the children, Dasharatha felt very happy.

Meanwhile the four children had grown up and Dasharatha started discussing their marriages. At that time, Vishwamitra came to the palace. On hearing the news, the security guards ran to the king and told about the arrival of Vishwamitra. Dasharatha felt very happy and went out to welcome him in. After the greetings were exchanged, Dasharatha expressed his gratitude for arriving at his palace. He said that his life was fulfilled with Vishwamitra's arrival. He tried to ask the reason for his arrival to the palace. He promised him that he would make Vishwamitra happy in any case.

On hearing the words of Dasharatha, Vishwamitra said that he would fulfil his words into actions if he was an honest king. Vishwamitra said to Dasharatha that he had started Yagna for the benefit of the world but it was being disturbed by Raakshasas. They were two evil spirits named Marichasu, Subaahu. They were throwing blood and meat into Yagna's platform. He said that he could not continue the yagna due to them. He wanted to curse them but during the yagna, it would not be good to get angry. So he came to Ayodhya to take Srirama for the protection of the yagna and to kill Marichasu and Subahu. He said that only Srirama could do that as he was a very good warrior and was praised in three worlds. He said that everybody was hesitating to come and protect the yagna.

Vishwamitra told Dasharatha not to reject his request, keeping the love on the eldest son, Srirama. He said that Dasharatha was a disciple of Vashishta and he knew that he would be on his word.

He asked the ministers to send Srirama with him. He told that he needed the aid of Srirama for ten nights. If he was cooperative for ten nights, his yagna would resume without any disturbances. He suggested Dasharatha not to be unhappy within. He promised that Srirama would come back to the kingdom.

Dasharatha replied that his son was only just fourteen years old and he was not eligible to fight. Dasharatha said that he would come and kill the rakshasas in the place of Srirama. But he said that he was not ready to send his son. In case if anything would happen to Srirama, he would not bear the pain. Srirama was not good at expecting the strength of enemies.

Dasharatha told Vishwamitra instead of taking Srirama who was just fourteen year old, he would take Dasharatha who was sixty thousand years old. He continued, he would get Srirama after so many years of waiting. And Srirama was very dear to him. He said that he would not live without Srirama.

Then, Vishwamitra told Dasharatha that Marichasu and Subaahu were provoked by Ravana and disturbing the yagna. Dasharatha intervened and told even Gandharvas had been defeated by Ravana. How Srirama would kill them, it wouldn't be possible for him.

So he stated that he was not sending his son. Instead he would come and engage in war with Marichasu and Subaahu. On hearing that Vishwamitra got angry with Dasharatha. Vishwamitra said that Dasharatha had promised him and he told that he would do anything for him at the beginning. With Vishwamitra's rage all the gods were terrified and the earthquake occurred.

Then Vashishta Maharshi intervened and told Dasharatha that it would not be good to take back the promise. No one in the Ikvakshu family had taken back the promise they had given to others before. He reminded them of the greatness of their family and about him. If Dasharatha had taken back his promise, it would be a sin and something terrible would happen. He said that Srirama was a great warrior and there were no war skills that he had not known. And rakshasas would do anything.

Vishwamitra himself was a universal guru and he knew everything. In fact Vishwamitra was greater than him. He would teach more skills to Srirama. He suggested Dasharatha not to be hesitant to send Srirama with Vishwamitra. With the convincing words of Vashishta Maharshi, Dasharatha was pleased and agreed to send his son, Srirama with Vishwamitra. Later he called Srirama and told him to go with Vishwamitra to protect his yagna. Srirama obeyed his father's instruction.

In the presence of Vashishta and Kausalya, Dasharatha handed Srirama over to Vishwamitra.

While Srirama was accompanied by Vishwamitra, all the gods from heaven blessed him. While they all bid farewell to the forest, the court musicians played auspicious and melodious music. Laxmana who always accompanied him, went with Srirama to the forest. They travelled for a few miles to the south. They reached the bank of the river Sarayu. Then Vishwamitra spoke to Srirama, "I would teach you sacred powerful mantras. Repeat them after me. After you had uttered the mantras, you would get powerful warrior skills. You wouldn't get exhausted and get a fever with the mantras. Nobody would kill you during your sleep.

With the mantras nobody could beat you"

Srirama felt very happy and he was ready to learn them. When Vishwamitra was chanting, he repeated after him. Later Srirama could become more confident and could become a great warrior. In the night, they slept on the bank of river Sarayu while Vishwamitra was singing melodious songs. This was the first time Srirama and Laxmana were sleeping on the grass. All these days they slept on the soft bed in their palace.

When the day broke, Vishwamitra was speaking to Srirama and Laxmana who were sleeping on the dried grass. He told them to wake up and to take bath in the river as they had to perform puja before the sun rose. They immediately woke up, took a bath and performed puja as Vishwamitra said. Later they took blessings of him and resumed their journey.

While they were going, they encountered the Ganges River and the ashrams. On seeing the river and ashram, Srirama and Laxmana were dumbfounded to see the river's beauty. And they asked Vishwamitra about the peaceful ashrams, located on the bank of the river Ganges.

Srirama and Laxmana asked Vishwamitra, "Who lived in the ashrams Guru?"

Then Vishwamitra told them, "Lord Shiva used to do meditation and after the meditation, he married goddess Parvathi. Later they started to go to Kailasa. While Lord Shiva and Goddess Parvathi were going to Kailasa, Manmadha encountered and blocked their path. When Lord Shiva was singing Omkaram, all the body parts from Manmadha were separated and burnt. From that day onwards, Manmadha was called the epithet of cupid. The place later was revived as the sacred ashram"

Later, Vishwamitra to them that they were going stay that night and the following morning their journey would resume in between the Ganges and the Sarayu. That night, all the saints, who were living in the ashrams, entertained Srirama and Laxmana with enchanting songs and stories. The eldest, Kaushika Maharishi, told them stories of the gods'.

Next morning, Srirama and Laxmana followed Vishwamitra to the river bank. At the river bank, all the saints made a boat for them to travel in the river. Later they got into the boat and travelled in the river. They heard a strange sound in the middle of the river. Then Srirama asked him what the sound was. Then Vishwamitra told him, "Once Lord Brahma made a lake on the mount of Kailasa. The water flowed to Ayodhya. Since the river was formed due to the water of the lake, the river was named as Sarayu. And the water of Sarayu merged with the Ganges. During the merging it made a sound. That was the sound you heard"

Srirama and Laxmana saw the dense forest, while they were travelling in the boat. They questioned Vishwamitra about the forest. Then Vishwamitra said, "They are Maladha and Karoosha countries. In these counties, raakshas live. There is a giant lady named Thataaka. She has the power of a thousand elephants. She has always been amorous on men. Marichudu is her son and he is always threatening the people with his voice and strength. And he is destroying the property of the people. In a few miles we are going to reach the entrance of the Thataaki's forest. They may encounter us and block our path" So he told Srirama to kill them with his archery skills.

Srirama told Vishwamitra, "I have immense respect for you. My father is a great king and he told me to listen to you. I definitely do whatever you order me to do. My father helps the people in many ways. In the same way, I will be helpful to the Brahmins in these countries by killing Thaataki. I will do anything for the welfare of this country"

Immediately he took his bow into his hands and started aiming at the enemy. When he dragged and let loose the thread, it produced a great sound. On hearing the sound, rakshasas in the forest were afraid. Thaataki comes to know that someone entered her forest and created terror among her fellow raakshasas. She came to the spot where Vishwamitra, Srirama and Laxmana were waiting for her.

On seeing the awkward form of her, Srirama told Laxmana, "Look! Laxmana how ferocious Tataki is and she has the biggest hearts. Even Yama will flee if he sees her physical appearance. Laxmana, I do not want to kill this giant since she is a lady. Instead I will cut her ears and nose to lessen her strength. And I will make her unable to walk further." On hearing this, Thaataki came forward, lifting her giant hand to beat Srirama. While she was coming forward, Vishwamitra blessed them to fight with her and win.

Thaataki, who was ferocious, created the gale, which made Srirama and Laxmana terrified. She threw big stones on them. Srirama, who got angry with her, stopped the flow of stones with his arrows. Later he aimed his arrows at her hands, resulting in her two hands being cut off. She fell down onto the ground, crying. Laxmana went to her and cut off her ears and nose. Then she changed into many forms and again threw stones at them in disguise without being noticed.

Then Vishwamitra told Srirama, "Do not show sympathy to her. She is a wicked woman and has a dangerous history. So do not hesitate to kill her before the sun sets. Otherwise she would disturb our yagna. Then Srirama took his bow and started aiming at her with his arrows. Immediately Thaataki was changing into many forms to confuse Srirama. And she came face to face with him. Without being late, Srirama shot an arrow into the breast of Thataki. With that she fell onto the ground and died. There was a shower of flowers from heaven and the gods appreciated Srirama's act. All the gods suggested Vishwamitra to learn more skills as he needed to do many tasks further. So Vishwamitra went to Srirama and started saying something in his ear. After Srirama had killed Thaataki, Vishwamitra suggested that he stay back there that night. They spent that night happily in the forest. The forest itself thrilled as it had got redemption from the curse after the ages. It seemed as if it was Kubera's garden. All the gods felt happy with Srirama that night.

Next morning, Vishwamitra told Srirama, "I am very happy for what you have done. So I want to teach you more archery skills" He taught all the skills to Srirama. Even the skills felt very happy for they are going to be used by Srirama. Later he received them with utmost care and happiness. Everyone was very happy for Srirama there.

Later they started their journey. While they were travelling, Srirama asked, "I got the different weapons from you. Would you please tell me how to use them?" Then the universal teacher of meditation, Vishwamitra taught how to use them. The arrows told Srirama, they were ready at any time to be used. When Srirama craves for them, they would appear before him. Later they disappeared.

Later they found a beautiful garden at a hill. The trees in it were dense like clouds. The birds, the animals and the flowers were pretty. Srirama and Laxmana asked Vishwamitra to tell them about it. Then he said, "The forest was very sacred. In this forest, Lord Vishnu had done meditation for many ages. This is the ashram of Vamana. This is the garden where I am performing the yagnas. They are being disturbed by the rakshasas. He told them that this was the place that Srirama had to kill them. Now we shall get into our ashram. Feel as if it is yours' ' While they were entering the garden, they shone like the star, Punarvasu.

On seeing Vishwamitra and two brothers, the saints in the ashram were on cloud nine. They adored Srirama and Laxmana apart from Vishwamitra. They had given very good hospitality to two brothers. Later they told them to take rest as they had to wake up in the early morning to protect the yagna. The next morning, Vishwamitra was about to commence the yagna. They slept in the ashram peacefully after having dinner.

Srirama and Laxmana asked Vishwamitra at what time the rakshasas would arrive to disturb the yagna. The saints, who were pleased with the two brothers, were getting ready for the fight with rakshasas. They appreciated the two brothers for their foresight. They said, "You have to take care of the yagna for next six nights' ' Vishwamitra, who remained silent as he started the yagna. Srirama and Laxmana were vigilant and they saw that there wouldn't be any disturbances.

After five days had been passed, Srirama told Laxmana that they had to be very careful. Since it was the last day, there might be an attack from the rakshasas. While they were discussing, the fire in the yagna's platform rose high and was shining with brightness. Everything was going on smoothly according to the customs and traditions. The sudden from the above terrified the people over there. The sound was like lightning and thunder. Marichasu and

Subaahu came there in disguise and created the blood flow to offend the yagna. Immediately Srirama and Laxmana tried to prevent the blood flow into the yagna. Later they identified the rakshasas in the sky.

Raakshasas discussed among themselves that they would kill Srirama and Laxmana easily since they were just human beings. Marichaudu told his fellows that he wouldn't degrade himself by killing the human beings. So he ordered them to kill Srirama and Laxmana, thinking that it was very easy for them. But Srirama aimed an arrow at Marichudu's heart and he fell into the water nearby. And the other arrow was aimed at Subaahu, with that he fell onto the ground in bleeding condition. The last was used to kill all the remaining rakshasas. All the rishis felt very happy with Srirama and Laxmana. They adored and revered them with flower garlands. Finally the yagna ended without any disturbances. Vishwamitra felt joyful as he ended the yagna as he planned. He also appreciated the two brothers.

Vishwamitra told Srirama and Laxmana, "You made Siddhashram significant. All the people over there prostrate to the sun that evening. Later they had their dinner and slept. Next morning Srirama had shown their gratitude for giving wonderful chance to be helpful for the sacred yagna.

Then all the rishis over there told Srirama and Laxmana that the king of Mithila Country was going to perform the yagna for the welfare of his people. So they said that they would go to the country as it was near the ashram. They told Srirama about Shiva's bow which was wonderful. If Srirama could come with them he could see the wonderful bow. Till now nobody has lifted it for the ages. If he came with them, he would see the yagna and try to lift the Shiva's bow.

Srirama and Laxmana agreed to go with them. Then all started their journey towards the north side. After they had travelled for some time, they reached the river Shona in the evening. They took bath in it and did puja. Then Vishwamitra started explaining about the country.

Kushudu was the son of Lord Brahma. He knew all the vedas and dharmas. He was adored by everyone in those days. He married the daughter of the king of Vidarbha. And she gave birth to four sons. Their names were Kushanabha, Kushambha, Asurtha Rajasa and Vasuvu. The fours were as great as their father, Kushudu. Since the four sons were warriors, Kushudu told them to rule his kingdom with following principles and morals.

The four sons listened to his father and started ruling the country by making four capitals. Kaushambi was the capital city of Kasubha, Mahodaya was Kushanabha's, Dharmaranya was surtha Rajasa's, Giripraja was Vesuvius. Vishwamitra continued, "See! (pointing to Srirama and Laxmana) Those are five mountains. Among the five mountains, a river is shining brightly like a garland which is made of beautiful flowers. The river, flowing to the east, is useful many of the farmers to yield crops"

Vishwamitra told Srirama and Laxmana, "Kushanabha married to Ghruthachi and they had hundred daughters. They were very beautiful like angels. Everyday they enter the beautiful garden to make it more beautiful. The hundred daughters are very good at singing, dancing and good at playing musical instruments. One day the god of air saw all of them and fell in love looking their beauty. He proposed that he would marry them. He told them that they would be treated as goddesses. He also told them if they lived like human beings, they would be mortal. If they married him, they would be immortal. Then the hundred daughters ridiculed him and rejected his proposal. They told that they were on meditation and they would abide by their father. Without his consent, they were not going to agree anybody's proposal. They told the god of air that their father was their god. Then the god of the air cursed them to be dwarfs. Instantly their bodies reduced to the size of span. They went to their palace with shyness. Their father, Kushanabha asked them angrily, "Who cursed you?" But they did not utter a word. The king was angry with them.

The hundred daughters touched their father's feet and told, "Father! the god of air tried to show his amourness to us. He talked to us in an immoral way. When we rejected his proposal of marrying us, he cursed us to become dwarfs. He did not listen even when we told about you"

Then the king felt very unhappy about what had happened with his daughters. But he felt very proud of them to stand on the righteousness and to revere their father. He told me that patience is a jewellery to a man or woman. He said that the gods have very less patience. He appreciated his daughters' behavior. Having patience and truth are almost equal to performing yagna. After having a discussion with his daughters, he told them to go.

Later Kushanabha discussed the marriage of his daughters with his ministers. He told them that he had to do his daughters' marriage as early as possible. Then the ministers told him about an auspicious man named "Choli". He was then doing meditation in the forest. A woman named, Somadha serving him. Somadha was the daughter of Urmila. After some days, Choli was satisfied with the work of Somadha. He asked her what she needed as a gift for serving him. She then craved for a son who is very intelligent since she didn't have husband. Then Choli blessed her with a son named Brahmadutta. Later Brahmadutta became the king of Kampilya. There he was treated as lord, Indra. So Kushanabha decided to give his daughters to Brahmadutta.

Later Kushanabha called Brahmadutta to his kingdom and did his daughters' marriage with him. When Brahmadutta touched the hands of all his daughters, they changed into their beautiful bodies. Then Kushanabha felt very happy with his daughters as they came out from the god of air's curse. Kushanabha and his wife welcomed them to their palace. Somadha also felt very happy to see her son becoming great by changing the fate of Kushanabha's daughters.

Vishwamitra continued the story. He said to Srirama and Laxmana, "Srirama! After Brahmadutta had got married, he did not have any offspring. So he started the yagna for wanting sons. While the yagna was going on, the son of Lord Brahma appeared and blessed him with a son. He said that Brahmadutta's son would be reputed as Gaadhi in the world. After blessing him, he went back to Brahma Loka.

As said by the son of lord Brahma, Gaadhi became very famous in the world. Vishwamitra said that he was the son of Gaadhi. On hearing this Srirama was surprised at the whole story of Vishwamitra's ancestors. Vishwamitra said, "Rama! Since I was born in the family of Kusha, I became

Kaushika. I have an elder sister, Satyavathi. She is a very honest woman and her husband's name is Rucheeka. After the death of Rucheeka, she went to heaven with him. In heaven she turned into a river on a hill. She is useful for the world by flowing her water. That is why, I am residing at this river. I used to love her very much. The love made me reside in her. Rama! You also helped me to live here permanently by slaughtering the rakshasas. This is the history of my dynasty"

That night they stayed on the bank of the river, Shona. In the morning, after they had finished ablutions and puja, they started their journey towards the river Ganges. They reached the Ganges by the evening. Srirama and Laxmana felt very happy on seeing the river Ganges. They took baths in the river and paid homage to their ancestors in the river. Later they sat beside Vishwamitra and asked the story of the river Ganges. Then Vishwamitra started narrating the story of the Ganges.

Vishwamitra said, "The River Ganges was the elder daughter of the mountains, Himavantha and Menaka. Umadevi was the Ganges' younger sister. One day, all the gods in heaven requested Himavantha to give his elder daughter for their necessities. Since the gods asked, he donated his daughter to them. Thus the sacred flowing Ganges went to heaven. Then Umadevi, the younger daughter of Himavantha did a great penance. Later she was married to Rudra" Vishwamitra told Srirama and Laxmana that the two daughters of Himavantha were sacred and adored by everyone in the world as well as in heaven.

Vishwamitra told Srirama and Laxmana, "Rama! Once, Lord Shiva married goddess Parvathi. Even after hundred years passed by, they did not get sons or daughters. Then all the gods went to lord, Shiva and told him that no one can wear his form. So only the mother earth can take the semen of him. Lord Shiva then agreed to give his semen. Later the gods requested the god of fire and the god of air to carry the semen to the forest on the earth. As a result of that, Kumara Swami was born. Kumara Swami became the son of the god of fire. There the Rishis worshipped lord Shiva and goddess Parvathi. Then they felt very happy to be worshipped.

Since gods requested lord Shiva, goddess Parvathi was angry and cursed all the gods that they would not get sons. She also cursed the mother earth that she would become a wife to many people. When the victims approached lord Shiva, he told them to travel towards the west. Then lord Shiva and goddess Parvathi started doing penance on the mountain of Himavath. Then Srirama and Laxmana understood the story of the Ganges.

While lord Shiva was doing penance, all the gods including Indra went to Lord Brahma and asked him for a leader. Then Lord Brahma created a son in the god of fire. That son became the leader of the gods. Then the gods requested Lord Brahma to drop the semen of lord Shiva in the Ganges.

Later the god of fire came to the Ganges and asked her to take the semen in her womb. Then the Ganges rejected the proposal of the god of fire. Then he requested her to leave the semen in the garden of Rellu. The Ganges did so then Karthikeya was born in the garden. Then the gods requested the soils to protect the son. They did so. Then the boy grew up in a day and he turned from Kumara Swami to Karthikeya. Vishwamitra told Srirama that whoever prayed to Karthikeya, they would be blessed with a hundred years of life. Apart from living in the world, they would also live with Karthikeya after their mortality.

Vishayamitra narrates the story of Sagarudu to Srirama and Laxmana. He told them that Sagarudu was the king of Ayodhya once. He was a very honest man and he too had no sons. His wife's name was Keshini who was the daughter of the King of Vidarbha. She was also an honest and righteous woman like her husband. Safaris had a second wife too. She was the daughter of the King of Aristanemi. Her brother's name was Suparnudu.

Sagarudu and his two wives had done penance on the mountain of Himavath. They did so for hundreds of years. Then Brugu Maharshi appeared and told them that they would be blessed with many sons. And they would become very famous in the world. The Maharshi said one of the wives would give birth to a son named Vamshankara and the other would give birth to sixty thousand sons. The the two wives asked the Maharshi who would get one son of them. Then the Maharshi asked them who wanted one son of great qualities and who wanted the sixty thousand sons.

Then the king Keshini craved Maharshi to give him one son who would be very great. But the second wife asked him to give her sixty thousand sons. Later the king came back to his palace with his wives. After a few months, the eldest wife gave birth to a son named Asamanjudu. And the second wife gave birth to bottle gourd. When they broke it, sixty thousand sons came from it. They brought the sons up in the pot of ghee. After a few years they all grew up and became young. The eldest son used to go to the river Sarayu with the other children. There they used to do mischievous things.

Since the eldest son was mischievous, the king banished

him from the country. The son, Amshumantha of Asamanju was a good warrior and liked by everyone in the world. After so many years the king had a desire to do yagna. So he immediately started it along with the priests who were good at Vedas.

Then Srirama asked Vishwamitra how Sagarudu had performed the yagna. Then Vishwamitra started telling about the yagna in detail. Rama! You know Lord Shiva was the son-in-law of the mountain of Himavath. The yagna was performed between the mountains of Himavath and Vindya. Sagarudu believed that the place was nice to perform the yagna. On the request of Sagarudu, Ashumantha got ready the horse for performing the yagna. But Indra, who saw the horse, stole it. So Sagarudu ordered Ashumantha to catch the thief and get the horse in time otherwise it would be a barrier to perform the yagna.

The king, Sagarudu also ordered his sixty thousand sons to search for the horse. They immediately started searching for it all over the world. But they did not find it. So they started digging the earth to know if it was beneath the earth. While they were digging the earth, many of the animals were killed by them. Then all the gods were afraid of the terrible thing and approached lord Brahma to save them. All the gods told what sixty thousand sons of Sagara were doing in the search for the horse.

Then lord Brahma told the gods that the mother earth is the wife of lord Vishnu. It was his responsibility to protect his wife. And lord Vishnu was in the avatar of Kapila Maharshi who was doing penance in the earth. The sixty sons who were digging the earth recklessly were cursed by Kapila Maharshi. On hearing the words of lord Brahma, all the gods went from the place.

The sons of Sagara were digging the earth with much force with their strong weapons. With this the mother earth was unable to bear the pain. They searched for the horse on the earth but they did not find it. Then they went to their father and told him that they had dug the earth and killed many animals but they had not found the horse. They asked their father what they had to do. Their father told them to find the horse not with their physical strength but with their wisdom. Their father ordered them to dig the earth once again. With that suggestion they started digging the earth with much more force. Digging much deeper, they reached the Pathala Loka. There they found the huge mountain. On the mountain an elephant was lifting the mother earth. When it tried to take rest, the mother earth moved slowly. The movement was treated as the earthquake. The sons circumambulated around the elephant and went in the direction of the east side. Later they went to the south. There they found another huge elephant named Mahapadma. It was the size of the mountain and it was also bearing the weight of the earth. Later they went to the west. There they found another elephant named Soumanasa. They also did circumambulation to it and went to the north. To their surprise, they found the fourth elephant named Bhadra. They knew that the four elephants were bearing the weight of the mother earth.

And there also the sixty thousand sons started digging the earth. Then they found Kapila Maharshi. On seeing him, they felt very happy. The horse which they were searching for, roaming there. They felt on seeing the horse, it was Kapila Maharshi who disturbed their yagna and started scolding him. Then they tried to attack Kapila Maharshi. Then the furious Maharshi cursed them. With the curse, they all were turned into ashes.

Sagarudu felt unhappy for returning his sons even after so many days. Then he called his grandson, Ashumantha. Sagarudu told his grandson that he was a very intelligent and good warrior. So he suggested that he take the sword as he would encounter the animals in the earth and search for the horse and the thief. He ordered his son to kill the thief who had disturbed their yagna by stealing the horse. He ordered at any cost the yagna would not be disturbed. It definitely had to be done. Ashumantha had gone beneath the earth through the way his fellow brothers had dug. There he saw a giant bird which was adored by the snakes. Then he asked the bird about the information of his fathers and about the thief who had stolen the horse.

The bird told him that he would take back the horse very soon. There he enquired every animal. They all said the same like the bird. Later he went to the place where his fathers had been burnt into ashes. He shed tears after seeing the heaps of ashes. There he also found the horse. Then he wanted to pay homage to his fathers. But he did not find any lake or river there. When he observed closely there, he found Garuthmantha who was the uncle of his fathers. Garuthmantha came to him and told not to cry. And he said that Kapila Maharshi had turned them into ashes. He also said that what he had done was the right thing. Garuthmantha suggested him to pay homage not with ordinary water but with sacred Ganges water. He told Ashumantha that the Ganges was the daughter of the mountain of Himavath. She only could get back their lives. And he told me to take the horse and finish the yagna. After his grandfather had finished the yagna, he could pay homage to his fathers.

Ashumantha, the great warrior, listened to the suggestion of Garuthamantha and had taken the horse to his kingdom. He told everything to his grandfather about what had happened on the earth with his fathers. His grandfather felt very sad on hearing the death news of his sons. Later he had finished the yagna on the suggestion of Garuthmantha. He later entered the town and tried to the Ganges to the earth to save his sons but he could not make it possible. Later he ruled the country for thirty thousand years and passed away.

After Sagarudu had died, the ministers made Ashumanthu as their king. He became very famous later in ruling. After a few years he gave his kingship to his son, Dilip and went up to the mountain of Himavath to do penance. He did it for thirty thousand years. There he joined the heaven choir. Later Dilip, who worried about his grandfathers' death, wanted to pay homage to the Ganges.

When he was worrying about it, he was blessed with a son named Bhaghiratha. Bhaghiratha was a very honest and virtuous man. Dilip ruled his kingdom for thirty thousand years and was demised. Dilip could not make it possible to get the Ganges to the earth. He was affected with some major disease and passed away. Due to the good deeds he did on the earth, he went to heaven. Though Bhaghiratha became the king, he did not get sons. So he gave his kingdom to his ministers and went on the work of taking the Ganges to the earth. He had done the major penance in the place of Gokarna. He did the penance in a variety of ways as no god appeared for his penance. Later he did that on a fast for a few years. In that way he had done penance for thousands of years.

Then lord Brahma felt very happy with the penance and appeared before Bhaghiratha. Lord Brahma asked what he had wanted. Then Bhaghiratha said that he wanted to pay homage with the Ganges to his forefathers as they had died by the curse of Kapila Maharshi. And he also craved for a son to continue his dynasty. Then lord Brahma said, "Bhaghiratha! You asked me what is not in my hands. If you want to get the Ganges, you can take the consent of lord Shiva. Since the Ganga is the longest and largest, it cannot flow from heaven. If it flows, the earth will be damaged due to its force of the flow. Only lord Shiva can wear the Ganges and he can take her to the earth" Later lord Brahma disappeared from the place.

After lord Brahma had disappeared, Bhaghiratha did the penance again standing on his toe for a year. Lord Shiva liked the penance and appeared before him. Shiva asked him what he wanted. Then Bhaghiratha told his desire of the Ganges to pay homage to his grandfathers. Then Shiva agreed to wear the Ganges and promised him that he would make it possible to take the Ganges to the earth. Later he ordered the Ganges to flow onto the earth from heaven. When the Ganges started flowing onto the earth with much more force, lord Shiva stood to receive it on his hair. The Ganges felt that it would even take lord Shiva to Pathala Loka with its force. The Ganges became egoist, feeling that it had much force. Then lord Shiva imprisoned the Ganges in his hair and made it so that it would not be seen by anyone. Later the Ganges was settled suffocating within Shiva's hair. Then Bhagiratha prayed to lord Shiva to release the Ganges so that he would pay homage to his forefathers with it.

Vishwamitra continued telling the next part of the story to Srirama and Laxmana. After getting satisfied with Bhaghiratha's penance, lord Shiva dropped the Ganges into the lake of Bindu from his hair. Then the river Ganges divided into seven parts. Hradini, Pavani, Nalini were the parts that flowed to the east with the auspicious water. Suchakshuvu, Sita, Sindhuvu were the parts that flowed to the west. The seventh part flowed behind Bhaghiratha. That is why the seventh part of the Ganges was called Bhaghirathi. While Bhaghiratha was travelling in his chariot, the seventh part of the Ganges followed him. When the Ganges came to the earth, a very big sound occurred. And the earth was filled with many animals like tortoises, fish etc.. Then the earth looked much more beautiful.

Apart from the animals, the gods also came onto the earth. With their arrival the earth shone like a beautiful planet. The sun and the moon looked more beautiful than before. Fish and the other animals were freely swimming in the Ganges. The sky laughed looking at the Ganges' flow. Even the clouds were happy to absorb its water and they looked white. The river Ganges flowed straight at one place, in a curved shape at the other place. It was flowing differently at different places. After the Ganges had started flowing on the earth, it became sacred and lost its sins.

When people, Rishis and the kings knew that the Ganges was flowing on the earth, they all came to the place where it was flowing and took bath in it to lose their sins. All the Rishis, people and the kings followed the chariot of Bhaghiratha to touch the Ganges. All of them felt very happy on seeing it on the earth. The Ganges flows behind the chariot of Bhaghiratha.

While Bhaghiratha and the Ganges were going to the spot where his forefathers had been burnt into ashes, Jahnuvu Maharshi was doing the yagna. The things of Jahnuvu Maharshi were swept away in the Ganges. Then Jahnuvu got furious and swallowed the whole Ganges. On seeing this episode everyone who were following felt dumbfounded. They all praised Jahnuvu and requested him to release it as it was equal to his daughter. Then Jahnuvu's angry subsided and released the Ganges. That is why the Ganges was also called as Jahnavi and Jahnusutha. Later they reached the Pathala Loka. Bhaghiratha requested it to flow on the ashes' heap of his forefathers. When the Ganges flowed, all of them reached heaven.

Later lord Brahma appeared before Bhaghiratha and told him, "You made it possible to send sixty thousands of your forefathers to heaven by making it possible to take the Ganges to the earth. Since you took the Ganges to the earth, it became your daughter. The Ganges is also treated as the Bhaghirathi that is in your name. It is also treated as the Ganges, Divya and Bhaghirathi since it travels in three routes. So now you can pay homage to your forefathers here and fulfil your ambition. Many people of your dynasty died without fulfilling their desire. Now you have the wonderful opportunity to pay homage to your forefathers. You will be revered in the world for the great thing you have done. What is not possible for others, you made it possible. So you became a virtuous man. Now go and take a bath in the Ganges. Then you will get virtue and get good results forever" Saying these words lord Brahma disappeared.

After lord Brahma had disappeared, Bhaghiratha paid tribute by doing Pinda Pradhan to the departed souls. He took bath in the Ganges and went to his kingdom to rule. There he was revered by everyone for his honest and sincere rule. Thus the story of the Ganges was told to Srirama and Laxmana by Vishwamitra in detail. He told whoever tells or listens to the story of the Ganges, their life will fulfill their desires and will become virtuous. And their sins will turn into good acts. Vishwamitra told them that since it was approaching dusk, they were suggested to take bath and perform the puja.

While Vishwamitra, Srirama and Laxmana were travelling, Srirama saw a town. He immediately asked Vishwamitra to tell the history of it. Then Vishwamitra started explaining about the town. Once there lived two strong men named the sons of Dithi and the sons of Adithi. Those were very energetic and proud at the war. The two people had a desire that they would live as the young forever. They thought that they would churn the sea of milk. To churn it, they went to the king of snakes, Vasuki to act him as the thread. Vasuki agreed to their proposal. Then they could arrange the mount of the hibiscus in the middle of the sea. Later they started churning it. After a thousand years, Vasuki started vomiting the poison. The poison was very powerful even the stones melted with it.

By and by, more poison was coming out of it. The poison was like a fire that no one could bear. With it slowly the area started burning. All the gods thought that the whole world would perish if it continued to come out. So they approached lord Shiva to protect it from the dangerous poison. Later they went to lord Vishnu and prayed before him to save them. Then lord Vishnu told lord Shiva in this way. Oh Shiva! When the gods were churning the sea of milk, the poison came first. The poison was the thing which related to you. So I request you to receive the poison and save the gods. Later lord Vishnu disappeared from the place. To save them, lord Shiva went to the place and swallowed the whole poison as if it was ambrosia. After saving them, lord Shiva disappeared from there.

Later the gods again started churning it. After a few years, the mount of hibiscus which was acting as churning staff, slid down to the Pathala Loka. Then all the gods again approached lord Vishnu and prayed before him to save them. Then lord Vishnu changed into the tortoise and went beneath the sea. Later lord Vishnu lifted the mount of hibiscus.

He stayed there for a thousand years until the gods churned the sea. Later he came out. Along with him so many angels came out. The angels were about sixty crores. Though they came out, no one craved for them so they remained as prostitutes. Then the wine started coming out of the sea but no one drank it. So the gods preferred to drink it. They felt very happy later drinking it as it made them drowsy.

Later the horses and some other creatures came out the sea as a result of churning. Finally ambrosia came out of it. The rakshasas and the gods fought for it. A great war between them. Later lord Vishnu appeared in disguise and stole it to prevent it from the rakshasas. Later the sons of Diti and Adithi were killed in the war. Later all the gods drank the ambrosia and they became ever younger. After they had been killed lord Indra started ruling the place.

Dithi felt very sad for her sons being killed in the war. She spoke to her husband Kasyapa that their sons were brutally killed by the gods. So she craved for a son who would kill lord Indra. She told her husband that she was going to do penance for wanting a great son. Kasyapa, who understood his wife's pathetic situation, gave her permission to do penance. He gave a boon that she definitely would get the son who would kill lord Indra. But she would be sacred for at least a thousand years if her desire wanted to be fulfilled. After blessing her, he left the place. Later Dithi did the terrible penance at Kushalava with a lot of zeal.

With her dedication, lord Indra provided her what she needed to do the penance like firewood, fruits, stems. Later lord Indra came in disguise and started pressing Dithi's legs to relieve her from the strain. Her meditation was about to complete in ten years. So she felt very happy that her meditation was going to complete and her wish was going to be fulfilled. That afternoon she slept keeping her head at feet side happily without knotting her hair. So lord Indra treated her as a sacred lady and he felt happy.

Next lord Indra entered Dithi's womb in the micro form and cut off the embryo into seven pieces. Since he was using his diamond weapon while cutting, the baby started crying loudly. With this Dithi woke up from the sleep. Lord Indra ordered the baby not to cry but the baby did not listen to him. So he cut it into small pieces. Dithi who knew this, what was happening in her womb, requested lord Indra not to cut off the baby. Later the baby came out from her womb. Then lord Indra also came out and told her that he had cut off the baby since she slept in reverse. He cut off the baby into seven pieces for a valid reason. The seven pieces of the baby would conquer lord Indra in the war. Later he apologized for doing so.

Thus Vishwamitra told Srirama and Laxmana several stories how lord Shiva and Parvathi cursed the mother earth, how Bhaghiratha brought the Ganges to the earth and the story of the sea of milk.

After her baby was cut off into seven pieces, Dithi felt very unhappy. She told lord Indra that it was her fault. Due to the sleeping on the wrong side, he had to cut off the baby. So she agreed that it was not the mistake of Lord Indra. So she requested lord Indra to do her a favour. She told him to make the seven pieces as leaders of the place for the air. These babies would always roam in the air and make them as Maruthas in the sky.

One in the brahma loka, second in the Indra loka, third in Divya loka and the rest four became the leaders of the four directions. These were known as the Maruthas. Lord Indra agreed to whatever she desired that would become true. He promised her that her sons would be known as the gods.

While traveling Vishwamitra had shown to Srirama and Laxmana the place, Kakusta where Dithi had done meditation. Since Vishala was born to Ikshvaku and Alambusa, the place was known as Vishala too. At this place the town Vishala was constructed by the Ikshvaku dynasty.

The son of Vishala was Hemachandra. Hemanchandra's son Suchandra, Suchandra's son Dumrashwa, Dumrashwa's son Srunjaya, Srunjaya's son Sahadeva, Sahadeva's son Krushashwa, Krushashwa's son Somadutta, Soma Dutta S son Kakusta, now the son of Kakusta Sumati is ruling the town, said Vishwamitra.

The kingdom is being ruled by Sumati in a well manner and all the people were happy with his rule, Vishwamitra told

Later Vishwamitra, Srirama and Laxmana went to the town of Vishala. There they were greatly welcomed by the king. The king and the courtiers were astonished to look at the princes Srirama and Laxmana. They said that the princes were looking like the sun and the moon. Later Vishwamitra introduced Srirama and Laxmana to the king and the courtiers. On knowing about them, Sumati felt very happy to come to their kingdom. Later he prostrated to them. There Vishwamitra, Srirama and Laxmana spent that night.

And in the morning they started for the town of Mithila. On seeing the town Srirama felt very happy. The town was very beautiful. There they saw an ashram. Srirama enquired about the ashram.

When Srirama asked about the ashram, Vishwamitra started explaining the narrative of Ahalya. Once this ashram belonged to Gauthama. The ashram was even adored by the gods in those days. Gauthama had done the meditation along with Ahalya. The meditation was done at different stages for many years. One day knowing the absence of Gauthama Muni, lord Indra disguised as Gauthama Muni and came to the ashram. Ahalya thought that lord Indra to be her husband since he looked exactly like her husband. Lord Indra asked Ahalya for intercourse. Since it was not the right time, Ahalya had a suspicion of him and later she found that he had lord Indra. But she would not prevent lord Indra showing his amorousness to her. Later they engaged in intercourse. Next she suggested that he leave the ashram without being noticed by anyone. And she said if her husband saw her, he would kill her.

Then lord Indra replied to Ahalya that he had felt very happy with her. And he started going out. Suddenly he encountered Gauthama Muni at the entrance of the ashram. Gauthama Muni usually was very powerful even when he opposed gods if they were unlawful. Raged Gauthama Muni, scolded and cursed lord Indra for acting like him in his form. Lord Indra was very afraid of Gauthama Muni with his anger. Gauthama Muni cursed him like a man without testicles.

Instantly the testicles of Lord Indra fell onto the ground. Later he also cursed his wife, Ahalya by making her stone in the mud where she had slept with lord Indra. When she requested, Gauthama gave her an exemption that she would get redemption when Srirama comes to the ashram after thousands of years. Since Gauthama was very powerful, the people who would pray to him, they would be free from all the seven sins: lust, greed, gluttony, pride, envy, anger and sloth. So Srirama went and prayed for him. Later Srirama, Laxmana and Vishwamitra slept on the mountain.

Later lord Indra approached the god of fire and the other gods. He told them what had happened in the ashram. He explained in fact he went to disturb his meditation as a result he became a victim. He told them that Ahalya was also punished because of his mistake. So he requested them to get back testicles. All the gods listened to lord Indra and they could arrange the testicles of a sheep to lord Indra. Since then our forefathers were only eating the goats without testicles. So Vishwamitra tried to explain the greatness of Gauthama Muni.

Later Vishwamitra took Srirama into the place where Ahalya had been cursed as the stone. Srirama and Laxmana entered the place following Vishwamitra. When Srirama's feet touched the stone, it turned into human being, Ahalya. When she changed into human form, the place shone brighter. Now Ahalya was free from her curse and looking more beautiful than before.

Srirama and Laxmana took the blessings of her and she took their blessings. When this happened, the rain of flowers showered the place. The gods celebrated the occasion. Everyone adored Ahalya. Later Gauthama Muni also felt very happy with Ahalya. Thereafter they lived happily in the ashram.

Later Srirama, Laxmana and Vishala went to the town of Mithila. From there they reached the spot of yagna. The king of Mithila, Janaka welcomed and appreciated them. Later they built a small hut to live on the bank of the river. Later Janaka took Shathanada to the yagna place to be helpful to Vishwamitra. Then Vishwamitra received the provisions required for the yagna from them. Later he enquired about Janaka's kingdom.

Janaka replied that everything was going nice. He prayed to Vishwamitra along with his priests. Then Vishwamitra was seated on the platform to start the yagna. Later they finished it successfully. Janaka felt very happy for completing the yagna successfully. He showed his gratitude towards Vishwamitra. Vishwamitra told him to be on fast for twelve days. Then it would be successfully completed.

Janaka asked Vishwamitra about the two princes. These people are looking very bright and pretty. Then Vishwamitra told him that those were the sons of Dasharatha. Vishwamitra told him that they had come to rescue his yagna from the rakshasas and they killed them. While coming there, they fulfilled many of their duties like changing Ahalya. And he took them to show the bow which was Janaka. Then Shatananda, the priest of Janaka started telling the history of Vishwamitra.

Once, Vishwamitra was a philanthropist, very well educated and the killer of enemies. He was king for many years. Vishwamitra was the son of Gaadhi. Gaadhi's father was Kushanabha and Kushanabha's father was Kushudu. After Vishwamitra ruled thousands of years, he decided to go around the world in a chariot. Thus he visited many rivers, states, towns, mountains and ashrams. Finally he ended his tour and reached the ashram of Vashishta. The ashram was beautiful and full of flowers, fruits and different kinds of animals. Apart from the animals, Rishis and gods used to visit the ashram.

Vishwamitra was equal to the position of Brahmarshi, the god of fire and lord Brahma. Because he used to take water, air and fire as food. And sometimes he used to depend on fruits, roots and stems. He had conquered over the senses and had not any fault. When Vishwamitra performed any yagna, all the gods used to be present. Thus the ashram was called Brahma Loka-II.

Vashishta welcomed Vishwamitra and his army. Later Vishwamitra and Vashishta discussed for a while in the ashram. In the ashram, Vishwamitra was adored by Vashishta and his disciples. He provided all types of fruits and stems to Vishwamitra. Since Vishwamitra was satisfied with the hospitality of Vashishta, he asked Vashishta to provide delicious food. Vashishta promised that he would provide any kind of delicious food to everyone that they exactly liked. Then Vishwamitra gave him the list of different cuisines like chutneys, rasam, rice and all types of vegetable curries.

Vashishta prayed for Kamadenuvu and it appeared before him. Then he asked all types of cuisines to the people over there whatever they liked to have. Then it created immediately whatever had been asked. Some of the food it gave were honey, sugar cane juice, cereals, pastry dishes, rice, curd, sweet, hot etc.. Everybody had had them all as they were delicious. After having them, everybody became very strong. Women, priests, ministers, and servants felt very happy. Then Vishwamitra asked Vashishta to give him Kamadenuvu, in place of it, he agreed to give him one lakh of cows. Since the cow was sacred, that had to be at the king. Vishwamitra requested him to think righteously.

Then Vashishta replied that he was not ready to give Kamadhenu even Vishwamitra was ready to give one crores of the cows. I would keep it with myself but do not give it to anyone else, said Vashishta. The cow was very sacred and I am paying homage to my forefathers with it, he said. Apart from that, all the yagnas depended on the cow.

Thus Vashishta rejected his proposal. Then Vishwamitra took all of his gold and he was even about to give a thousand elephants. And he was ready for horses, golden chariots and one crore cows. But Vashishta did not agree to give it. Vishwamitra tried to convince him to the maximum but his attempt would turn futile. Finally Vashishta agreed to give Kamadhenu on one condition. If Vishwamitra was ready to give his cow named Shabala, he would give Kamadhenu. But Vishwamitra told that the cow, Shabala, was everything to him and he said that he was not going to give it to anyone.

Since Vashishta did not agree to give Kamadhenu, Vishwamitra tried to take the cow with force. Vashishta was in grief as Vishwamitra was dragging the cow. Then the cow started crying why it was being dragged, what mistake it had made. It cried saying what kind of sin it had committed. It proclaimed that it was a sacred devotee. It asked Vashishta why he had given it to Vishwamitra. Then it started praying to all the gods to save it from Vishwamitra.

Vashishta told the cow that it was not his fault. Vashishta said, "Since Vashishta was the powerful king, I was unable to stop him from taking you. He was taking you with force, though I refused. Since he was the king, I would not protest.

He had a powerful army. That made me to prevent him"

Then the cow listened to Vashishta patiently. And it said that the strength of Brahmin was more powerful than the strength of Kshatriya. So Vashishta was more powerful than Vishwamitra.

Then it asked him if he was afraid of him. It immediately raged on Vishwamitra and created the great army which was more powerful than his. The army tried to kill everyone related to Vishwamitra. On seeing that, Vishwamitra was horrified.

Raged Vishwamitra started encountering the army of Vashishta. Then the cow again created a terrible man named Shaku. Shaku could easily defeat the army of Vashishta, with his warrior skills. Within a short period, the army of Vishwamitra was killed by him. Then Vishwamitra created his Divyasthra to encounter the army of Vashishta.

The Divyasthra started spoiling the army of Vashishta. Then Vashishta was disappointed and asked Kamadenuvu to recreate the strong men who are equal to the sun and the moon. Then it created two people and their names were Yavan and Shaku. These strong people killed the army of Vishwamitra in two minutes. All of Vishwamitra's animals and soldiers were killed by them. The hundred sons of Vishwamitra got angry with Vashishta and tried to attack him.

The furious Vashishta encountered them strongly and killed them in a few minutes. They were all turned into ashes with the curse of Vashishta. On seeing the deaths of his sons and army, Vishwamitra went into depression. He came to know the greatness of Vashishta and the cow. He became as if the bird without wings, the waves without speed, the snake without fangs and the sun without light.

Later Vishwamitra went to the mountain of Himavath, where he had done meditation for the blessings of lord Shiva. After a few years, lord Shiva appeared before Vishwamitra and asked what he wanted. Then Vishwamitra asked to tell him the secrets of Dhanurveda. With that blessing, Vishwamitra would get different asthras of gods and rakshasas. Lord Shiva blessed him with all of his desires. As a consequence of this, he became very powerful.

Vishwamitra got furious with Vashishta then as he became very powerful. His vanity made him go to Vashishta ashram to attack him. On one full moon day, Vishwamitra went to the ashram of Vashishta and showed his power before him. With the strength of Vishwamitra, the ashram turned into ashes. On seeing that, all the people there were afraid of Vishwamitra.

The disciples and the animals in the ashram fled away to safer places. Within a few seconds the ashram became like a serene desert. Then Vashishta got angry at Vishwamitra and took an oath that he would smash Vishwamitra for his wicked act. He felt very unhappy for his ashram which had been brought up by him over the years. Then Vashishta took out his Brahmasthra to kill Vishwamitra.

Vishwamitra, who saw Vashishta taking his Brahmasthra, took his Northwest asthra to beat him. Vashishta challenged Vishwamitra to show his power before him. He proclaimed that the power of Brahman was greater than the power of Kshatriya.

When Vishwamitra shot his asthra of northwest, it failed before the Brahmasthra of Vashishta. Then Vishwamitra used all of his powers which he gained with blessings of lord Shiva on Vashishta. But all the asthras failed before Brahmasthra. Even the gods were afraid of the Brahmsthra when it was experimented on Vishwamitra's. After making Vishwamitra's asthras powerless, Vashishta swallowed Brahmasthra. When it was done, he shone like the sun and became more powerful. Brahmasthra was looking like Yama's weapon-II.

Then all the gods requested Vashishta to calm down. Vishwamitra could know the power of Brahman and his vanity subsided with his ego. He came to know the power of Brahmsthra. It could easily make unsuccessful of his asthras. Later he had done another penance to turn into Brahman.

Unable to bear the pain of being defeated, Vishwamitra went in the south direction. He had done the terrible meditation with his wife taking only fruits and stems as his food. He had tried to conquer his senses and could succeed. Later truth and righteousness have become his prime principles. Later he was blessed with four honest sons and their names were Havishyandhudu, Madhushyandhudu, Drudanethrudu and Maharathudu. After thousand years of his terrible meditation, lord Brahma was happy with his meditation and appeared before him. Then he announced that Vishwamitra had not got the eligibility to become Brahman and disappeared. But due to his meditation, Vishwamitra later became Rajarshi. On hearing the words of lord Brahma, Vishwamitra was sulky and with grief.

Vishwamitra said to himself, "I had performed terrible meditation with utmost care but the gods recognised me as Rajarshi but not as Brahman " But later he was not discouraged and later he decided to perform the other penance. At that time, the king, Thrishanku of Ikshvaku dynasty decided to perform the yagna. His desire was to go to heaven in the human form. The king approached Vashishta and told his desire. Vashishta said that it was not possible for him. But without listening to Vashishta, the king went in the south direction. To fulfil his desire, he went to the sons of Vashishta. Then the sons of Vashishta were doing meditation for a long time. Then Trishanku saw them and felt very happy with their meditation.

Thrishanku saluted to them and told that he had decided to perform the yagna but he was rejected by their father. So he requested them to help in performing the yagna. They then said after he had been rejected by Vashishta, they were not ready to help as Vashishta was a great priest to the Ikshvaku dynasty. Even Vashishta was their father. They also rejected Thrishanku's desire to perform the yagna.

On listening to the words of Trishanku, the hundred sons of Vashishta got angry at Trishanku. They said that once he had been rejected by their father they too were not going to help him. They said that it was against to the nature. So they ordered him to go back to his town and stop trying the nonsense. No one would do the yagna for him except his father in the three worlds. Then Trishanku got angry at the hundred sons of Vashishta and told them that he would definitely approach someone and fulfill his desire of going to heaven in the human form. When the hundred sons heard that, they cursed Trishanku. Later they went to their ashram.

After two days of that incident, Thrishanku became a ruffian with the curse of the hundred sons of Vashishta. His body turned into black, ragged clothes, grey hair and was decorated with iron jewels. He looked exactly like a cemetery worker. On seeing his form, all of his ministers in the palace cursed and told him to leave the palace.

When Thrishanku went out, all the people saw him. They did not even look at him and fled. But he did not feel guilty and he approached Vishwamitra. When Vishwamitra saw him, he had shown sympathy for him as being a king, he turned into an awkward form. Later Vishwamitra inquired about the arrival of Trishanku. Then he told everything that had happened to him. He told Vishwamitra that he had performed many yagnas to reach heaven but it had not been possible for him. He told Vishwamitra that he had ruled his kingdom honestly and stood on righteousness. He made everyone happy but his fate had been turned into like that.

He also informed Vishwamitra that the Rishis were not happy with his yagna. He had not known why they were behaving like that. Then Vishwamitra replied to him that God was equal to everyone. To him, there were no religious differences. He consoled Trishanku saying his grief would definitely end. With his efforts, he unquestionably could satisfy the gods, said Vishwamitra.

Later Vishwamitra saw Thrishanku who was in the awkward form, and assured him that he would perform the yagna which he had been trying to do over the years to reach heaven in the human form. He also told him that he would call many virtuous Rishis and make it possible. Later Thrishanku could continue the yagna and could reach heaven in the awkward form, said Vishwamitra.

Vishwamitra continued, "King! Feel that the heaven is in your palm. Because you approached and sought help. You do not have to fear anybody. I will stand by your side" Later Vishwamitra told his sons to provide provisions which were required to perform the yagna. Later he ordered his disciples to prepare for the yagna. He also ordered his disciples not to refuse to follow, otherwise he told them that he would curse them. On hearing the words of their teacher, all of the disciples went in different directions to prepare for the yagna. Everyone agreed to come except the sons of Vashishta. When they were invited to the yagna, they cursed the disciples of Vishwamitra. After knowing that, a furious Vishwamitra cursed the sons of Vashishta. But they stood on their father's word that a Kshathriya was not eligible to do the yagna. But Vishwamitra told them if they disturb their yagna, they would turn into ashes. And they were taken to the Yama Loka. For seven hundred births, they would live as dogs and beggars. And they also become leprosy patients. Even the curse would apply to Vashishta, told Vishwamitra.

Later Vishwamitra came to know that Vashishta and his sons had died. Vishwamitra talked to the Rishis about the demise of them. He said that Thrishanku was one of the best kings in the dynasty of Ikshvaku. This man only will be going to heaven, Vishwamitra said.

Vishwamitra said to his fellow Rishis that they were going to perform the yagna. So everyone over there gathered at the place. Then they said that Vishwamitra, who belonged to the Kushiska dynasty, was very angry. They also talked among themselves that they had no other option except to listen to him. If they do not listen to him, they will also be turned into ashes, they talked. So they all decided to do the yagna to send Thrishanku to heaven.

Since Vishwamitra knew everything how to perform the yagna, all the Rishis who joined with him did the yagna according to traditions. They continued the yagna for several years and after that Vishwamitra invited all the gods to see the yagna. But the gods did not turn up to receive the hospitality of the yagna. Then Vishwamitra got angry at the gods and he told Trishanku in this way. "O king! Now I am sending you with this body to the heaven. As a result of the yagna, you have got the opportunity to go to the heaven. Now you go to the heaven" And he started going while the Rishis were watching him. lord Indra who saw Thrishanku coming to the heaven, said that he had no place to settle in the heaven. "So it is better to go back", lord Indra said.

When Trishanku was humiliated in heaven, he was falling onto the earth. While falling onto the earth, he prayed for Vishwamitra to save him. Then Vishwamitra who heard the crying of Trishanku, asked him to stop there in the sky. On witnessing the anger of Vishwamitra, the Rishis who laid in the south direction, created a constellation where Thrishanku was falling down. Then Vishwamitra said angrily that he was going to create another world and create another Indra. And he immediately started creating the gods as the substitution to fulfil the desire of Trishanku.

Then all the gods started requesting him to stop the creation of another world and the gods. They requested him that Thrishanku who had been cursed by Vashishta was not eligible to settle in the heaven. After listening to the gods' appeal, Vishwamitra decided to send Trishanku tin Vacuum where he created a constellation. He said that the constellation would be there permanently. He told the gods that they would make his oath into futile. Then the gods agreed to Vishwamitra's words.

Then between the earth and the heaven, there was another world named Vaishwanaramarga. There Thrishanku settled showing his head towards the earth and the legs to heaven. The stars over there were shining brightly. Till then Trishanku settled there. After the turmoil had been solved, all the gods and Rishis went to their respective places.

While the Rishis were going back to their ashrams, a terrible thing happened in the south direction. So Vishwamitra went in the direction of the west. There he found a sacred waterfall. At the waterfall he decided to stay and do meditation since the place was serene and very beautiful. At the place depending on the fruits and stems, he had done a great meditation. At that time the king of Ayodhya was Ambarishudu. While the king was doing the yagna, lord Indra stole the yagna's animal.

Then the priest who was doing the yagna, chided the king for his negligence for the animal. He suggested the king perform another yagna to prevent the mistake. He ordered him to bring back the stolen animal. If it had not been done so, he would have been punished for his negligence. The priest told the king that it was okay to take any human in the place of the animal. Then the king started searching for humans. Even the king was ready to give one crores of cows in replace of the human who was ready to participate in the yagna. While the king was searching for a human, he found a poor family on a hill. The head of the family was Ruchika Maharshi. Next the king went to him and asked for his son. The king said that he would give cows and gold. The king said that he had been in search of a human but he did not find one who was willing to participate. So the king requested him to give his son for the yagna.

Ruchika told that he had only three sons. He said that he was not willing to give his elder son. Ruchika's wife also rejected to give the last son. Usually the fathers love the elder sons and the mothers love younger sons. So the king asked the second son, Sunashepudu. Since he was the middle one, they agreed to give the king for the yagna. In return the king gave them a lot of gold, diamonds and one lakh of cows and took Sunashepudu to the yagna's place.

Later the king Ambarisha took Sunashepudu to the place where he had planned to perform the yagna. They were resting in the place before the yagna started. After some time they noticed Vishwamitra doing his meditation there. Vishwamitra was father-in-law of Sunashepudu. When Sunashepudu saw his father-in-law, he broke into tears as he was going to be slaughtered for the yagna. He directly went to Vishwamitra and fell in his lap and told him what had happened to him.

Sunashepudu said, "Uncle! You are only my saver now. You have saved so many people till now. The king believed in me so he took me here to complete his yagna. At the same time I want to live as I am too young to die. If you do not save me I will go to heaven at a young age. So you are only my lifesaver. Now I neither have a mother nor a father. I am nobody so please save me as if you are my father"

On knowing the pathetic condition of his nephew, Vishwamitra told, "The parents give birth to sons and they always feel that their sons live with abundant wealth and health. Now I have to save this young rishi" So Vishwamitra ordered his sons to join the yagna in place of the animal to save Sunashepudu. He also told them to please the god of fire so that his nephew will be saved. The barrier for the yagna will also be cleared. The gods will also be pleased"

Then all of Vishwamitra's sons including Madhuchandhu asked their father, "Do you want to kill your sons for the sake of the other's son?" And they disobeyed their father's order. Then Vishwamitra got angry with his sons and his eyes turned red. He ordered his sons to talk recklessly and it was the opposite of righteousness. The response of his sons disturbed him. He compared his sons with the sons of Vashishta. They too were as bad as his sons. Later He cursed his sons that they would live as beggars eating the meat of dogs for thousands of years.

Vishwamitra wore the garland of red flowers and applied red sandals all over his body. Later he told several mantras at the yagna pole and asked Sunashepudu to repeat after him and then the yagna would be resumed properly and he would live his life happily. After chanting the mantras, Sunashepudu told the king to be peaceful and to be on the fast for the yagna.

On hearing the words of Sunashepudu, the king, Ambarisha felt very happy and started the yagna. And with the permission of his family members and the people, he tied the animal which was worn red blooded clothes, tied to the pole. Later Sunashepudu repeated the mantras which were told by Vishwamitra to please the gods. Since Sunashepudu lauded lord Vishnu who was the younger brother of lord Indra, lord Indra was very much pleased and blessed him with long life. Later the king could complete the yagna without any disturbances. And the king was immediately blessed with many results. Later at the same place Vishwamitra had done his penance for one lakh years.

After a thousand years, all the gods came to Vishwamitra to bless him with a boon. Lord Brahma who was with glow, announced that Vishwamitra became Maharshi for his ages of austere penance. On hearing this, Vishwamitra felt very happy. Later lord Brahma went back to his loka. With enthusiasm, Vishwamitra Maharshi again started another penance.

While Vishwamitra was in his meditation, Angel Menaka arrived at the place to take bath in the water fall. While she was taking a bath, Vishwamitra was surprised to look at her beauty. As a result of that he was being distracted by his meditation. Unable to resist his lust, he welcomed her to his ashram. He said that he was distracted and had an amorous feeling on her. So he asked her to live with him. Thus his penance was disturbed.

Menaka stayed in the ashram with Vishwamitra for ten years. Later Vishwamitra came to know that the gods deliberately sent angel Menaka to disturb his penance. Since he had participated in intercourse with her, his penance had been disturbed. On knowing this, he was in grief. Later he told Menaka to leave the ashram. With the repent, he went in the north direction and there he started another penance. This time he would want to control all of his senses without being disturbed by anyone. On the bank of the river, Kaushika, he was doing his penance. With this gods felt afraid that if Vishwamitra gets more powers, their status can subside.

Later all the gods appeared before him and were honored with Maharshi. Lord Brahma spoke gently with Vishwamitra and appreciated for his continuous hard work. Then Vishwamitra requested Lord Brahma to make him Brahmarshi so that he would conquer his senses. Then lord Brahma said that he had not got the eligibility to become Brahmarshi. He said that he had to put more effort into achieving that. Later all the gods including Brahma disappeared from the place.

After the gods had gone, Vishwamitra had done the terrible penance without taking any food. He depended on air, fire and water as his food. This pleased the gods very much. But the gods were jealous of Vishwamitra so they tried to disturb his effort again.

All the gods requested lord Indra to disturb Vishwamitra's penance. Then lord Indra told Angel Ramba to disturb the penance of Vishwamitra with her beauty. But Ramba refused to do so since Vishwamitra was a very angry man. Then all the gods requested her to fear him. They said that they would save her in case of any mishap. "So go ahead, everything will be good", the gods said. Lord Indra also supported the gods. Finally he ordered Ramba to obey his instructions.

"A Cuckoo was singing, sitting on a branch of a tree in the month of Vaishaka. It was attractive to me. Accompanying Manmadha, I will be with you. With your beautiful dance, attract Vishwamitra. Behave as if you really wanted him" said Puruhutha.

Listening to Puruhita, Ramba tried to charm Vishwamitra. Vishwamitra saw her and felt very happy with her beauty. Meanwhile a cuckoo was singing melodiously on a branch. The singing of Cuckoo and the beauty of Ramba distracted Vishwamitra. Meanwhile his concentration on the penance had been disturbed. Vishwamitra guessed that it was lord Indra's technique. Raged Vishwamitra cursed Ramba for disturbing his conquest over the senses. So he called her a stupid and cursed that she would remain as stone for ten thousand years. After ten thousand years a sacred Brahman would turn her into an angel again. Since he got angry and lust, his trial became futile.

Immediately Ramba became stone. Later Manmadha went back from the place.
Vishwamitra was without peace later. So he took an oath

that he would not get anger, talk. He seriously decided to stand on his word until he became Brahman. That was an extraordinary oath he had never taken before.

Later Vishwamitra went in the direction of the east. There he had done a great penance for one thousand years. During his penance, he did not utter a single word. He had faced so many hurdles and became very weak during the penance but he did not lose his originality of having anger. He started eating food after the completion of a thousand years of his penance.

Then lord Indra came as a Brahman in disguise and asked for alms. Then Vishwamitra donated the rice which he cooked for himself without hesitation. Later he continued his penance without talking to lord Indra. Later Indra tried to disturb them by creating rakshasas but they died due to Vishwamitra's power. Then all the gods went to Brahma and told him that they had tried to disturb the penance but it was futile. Even though they tried he was becoming stronger and conquering all his senses. They said that they had not found any sin in him. If he becomes more powerful, he will burn the three worlds into ashes. On seeing his penance, the seas were crying, the mountains were spoiling, the mother earth was bearing pain. Even the wind was not blowing properly. The sun himself became dark before his power of light. They asked lord Brahma to save them from Vishwamitra.

Later lord Brahma went to Vishwamitra and said that all the gods were satisfied with his penance. So Brahma said that he was making Vishwamitra into Brahman and blessed him with eternal immortality. Then Vishwamitra felt very happy and told Brahma that he had some desires. He asked Brahma to fulfil them. Vishwamitra said, "Vedas should wear me. Vashishta should respect me. If you fulfill my desires, I will stop doing this penance" Later all the gods requested Vashishta to make friendship with Vishwamitra. He forcefully agreed to do that. Then Vishwamitra became Brahman and he was happy till then. Later the gods disappeared from the place.

Later Vashishta and Vishwamitra became friends and Vishwamitra roamed around the world. Thus Vishwamitra became Brahman. Then the king Janaka said that he was blessed to have the great person to perform his yagna. The king prostrated to him and said, "Since it was getting dusk, you can take rest and next morning you have to start the yagna" Later Vishwamitra, Srirama and Laxmana took rest in the palace.

Next morning, the king Janaka invited Vishwamitra, Srirama and Laxmana to his hall. There he felicitated them according to the traditions. He told them to accept his hospitality so that he would be very obliged. They accepted his felicitation later. Then Vishwamitra requested the king to show the bow of Shiva to Srirama and Laxmana since they wanted to see it. Vishwamitra told the king the greatness of them. "After watching it they would go back to Ayodhya", said Viswamitra. Then the king Janaka told the story why the bow of Shiva was with him.

The king, Janaka told, "The elder son of the emperor, Nimisha was Devaratha. Nimisha spoiled Dakshayagna then he found the bow of Shiva. He gave it to his son Devaratha to protect it. Later it was given Janaka by Devaratha. One day I was ploughing the field, I found a baby, Sita in the field. Many tried to marry Sita but I decided to give her to a hero who has all good qualities and warrior skills. Then the kings got angry with his proposal and forcefully entered the palace to take it away but it was not possible for any of them to at least lift it. So doing nothing, they went back to their places. Since they failed to lift and shoot it, I did not agree to give Sita to any of them. So they tried to invade Mithila, my country. For a year, the country faced so many struggles. We lived without proper food. Then I had done penance to please gods. Then the gods appeared and gave me full strength to defeat anyone. Later with my strength I defeated all of them and saved my country. Next the king told Vishwamitra, Srirama and Laxmana that he would show them the bow of Shiva. In case if Srirama lifts and shoot the bow and I can give Sita to him and do their marriage"

On hearing the words of the king, Janaka, Vishwamitra requested him that Srirama would try to lift it. Then the five thousand people lifted and moved to the hall keeping it in the big iron box. Then the king opened the box and showed it to them.

Later the king told about the bow in this way, "This is the most sacred bow and it was adored by our ancestors. Till now many of the great kings tried to lift and to brace the bow but no one could do that. Then the king told Vishwamitra to show it to Srirama. Then Srirama came and saw it. When he looked at it, his heart was thrilled. Next he touched it. When Srirama was observing it, the king told him to brace the bow. Then Srirama held the mid part of the bow. Thousands of people were watching the spectacular event. Without much effort, Srirama could easily list and braced the bow. When he did that, it broke into two pieces. Then all the people heard as if a thunder roared and the earthquake occurred. Many people fainted from the sound.

After some time the people woke up and then the king Janaka said in this way, "Oh! I was astonished on seeing the grandeur event done by the son of Dasharatha. The event was unprecedented. Now I can give my daughter Sita to

Srirama and do their marriage. My daughter will become the wife of Srirama and revive their dynasty. My daughter is everything to me in fact she is more than my life. If you permit me, I will send my ministers to Ayodhya in the chariots to inform the king, Dasharatha. And they will take his consent and bring him here. They will inform everything what has happened here"

After Vishwamitra had agreed, the king sent his ministers to Ayodhya. He ordered them to inform the king, Dasharatha and take him here.

The ministers of the king, Janaka, took three days to reach Ayodhya. On the way they slept at three places during the night. They reached the city with tired horses. They went into the palace and saw the old king Dasharatha. They saluted to the king and told him in this way, "The king of Mithila, Janaka sent us to you and he sent his regards to you. And with the permission of Vishwamitra, he sent us to inform you that Srirama has braced the bow of Shiva. Because of that, our king wanted to give his daughter to your son, Srirama. In that way he wanted to fulfil his promise which he did before your son had lifted and braced the bow. So he needed your permission for the marriage. And you are also invited to the occasion along with your priests and ministers"

Then the king, Dasharatha felt very happy and he immediately informed Vashishta, Vamana and his ministers. He informed them, "After Srirama had rescued Vishwamitra's yagna, he went to Mithila and there he lifted and braced the bow. With that, Janaka decided to send his daughter, Sita to Srirama. So they immediately have to start for Mithila without any delay"

On hearing the words of the king, Dasharatha, they all felt happy and told him they would start for Mithila the next morning.

Next morning, Dasharatha with all of his ministers and family members taking gold and money started for Mithila. He ordered his army to lead the road and Vashishta, Vamana and the other Brahmans would follow the army. Next he and his family would follow them in his chariot. As per the orders of the king, everything was prepared and they travelled for four days to reach Mithila.

The king, Janaka knew that Dasharatha and his people came to his city. So he welcomed them grandly. Janaka felt very happy on seeing the old king, Dasharatha and Vashishta Maharshi in his city.

When the king, Janaka looked at Vashishta, he looked like lord Indra. Janaka knew that the dynasty of Raghu revived because of him. He was very much obliged that his dynasty till now was also revived as his daughter was marrying Srirama. He told Dasharatha, "Oh! King, tomorrow you have to perform the marriage of your son with my daughter" The king Dasharatha asked the formalities as he was the father of the bridegroom and did everything according to the customs and traditions. Later everyone stayed in the palace happily. Later Srirama and Laxmana came to their father and touched his feet in the presence of Vishwamitra. The king was on cloud nine seeing his sons for a long time. Even the king, Janaka, was part of the happy moments that night.

Next morning, the king Janaka told his priest, Shatananda in this way, "You know my brother Kujadwaja was a prowess at the war. He is living in the city, Samikshya. Now I want to bring him here. He is my rescuer of the yagna. During tough times he was with me. Now I want to make him happy too" Then the priest told the soldiers to bring Kujadwaja to Mithila. Then they went and told him the reason for coming there. So with the invitation of his brother, Kujadwaja came to Mithila and received the hospitality of them.

The two brothers sat on the throne and ordered their minister Sudhamanudu to invite the king, Dasharatha. So he went to the place where the king, Dasharatha and his family were staying and invited to the hall on behalf of the king, Janaka. So, including Vashishta and Vishwamitra, all of them went to the hall.

Since Vashista was the teacher of Ikshvaku, with the permission of Vishwamitra, he spoke to the king, Janaka. He told the history of Dasharatha's forefathers before he asked for a bride to marry with Srirama as it was their tradition.

Then the king, Janaka saluted Vashista with two hands and told the history of their forefathers. He mentioned his father, Hraswaroma. He also talked about his brother, Kujadwaja's greatness. He shared with them how his brother became the king of Samikshya city. When Sudhanva tried to invade Mithila and marry Sita, his brother helped him and saved Mithila. Then the two brothers killed Sudhanva and he made his brother as the king of Sudhanva's kingdom, Samkashya. Janaka said that he had two daughters and he introduced his second daughter, Urmila. So they asked to marry Sita with Srirama and Urmila with Laxmana. They stated that their daughters were humble and honest. They requested Srirama and Laxmana to cut their hair and get ready for the marriage.

Vishwamitra and Vashishta spoke with Janaka in this way, "Ikshvaku and Videha dynasties are both unconquerable dynasties. Your brother, Kujadwaja has two daughters. So it will be very nice to give them to Bharatha and Shathrugna. They are also very nice boys like Srirama and Laxmana. And they are equal with Srirama and Laxmana in virtue and prowess at war" After listening to Vishwamitra and Vashishta, Janaka saluted to the king, Dasharatha and he said that his dynasty will be blessed if that happens. Since Vashishta and Vishwamitra were performing, the daughters of my brother were also blessed to have such virtuous boys.

Next morning, the king Janaka told his priest, Shatananda in this way, "You know my brother Kujadwaja was a prowess at the war. He is living in the city, Samikshya. Now I want to bring him here. He is my rescuer of the yagna. During tough times he was with me. Now I want to make him happy too" Then the priest told the soldiers to bring Kujadwaja to Mithila. Then they went and told him the reason for coming there. So with the invitation of his brother, Kujadwaja came to Mithila and received the hospitality of them.

The two brothers sat on the throne and ordered their minister Sudhamanudu to invite the king, Dasharatha. So he went to the place where the king, Dasharatha and his family were staying and invited to the hall on behalf of the king, Janaka. So, including Vashishta and Vishwamitra, all of them went to the hall.

Since Vashista was the teacher of Ikshvaku, with the permission of Vishwamitra, he spoke to the king, Janaka. He told the history of Dasharatha's forefathers before he asked for a bride to marry with Srirama as it was their tradition.

Then the king, Janaka saluted Vashista with two hands and told the history of their forefathers. He mentioned his father, Hraswaroma. He also talked about his brother, Kujadwaja's greatness. He shared with them how his brother became the king of Samikshya city. When Sudhanva tried to invade Mithila and marry Sita, his brother helped him and saved Mithila. Then the two brothers killed Sudhanva and he made his brother as the king of Sudhanva's kingdom, Samkashya. Janaka said that his brother also had a daughter named Urmila. So they asked to marry Sita with Srirama and Urmila with Laxmana. They stated that their daughters were humble and honest. They requested Srirama and Laxmana to cut their hair and get ready for the marriage.

So four sons of Dasharatha were about to marry the daughters of Janaka and Kujadwaja. Vashishtha and Vishwamitra decided to perform marriage on the auspicious star Uttarafalguni. Later Janaka offered the throne to Dasharatha.

After seated in it, Dasharatha spoke happily in this way, "The two brothers Janaka and Kujadwaja are virtuous and honest men. Everything will be fine with you. You prepare for marriage. I will pay homage to my forefathers meanwhile" Later Dasharatha went from the place.

After paying homage to his forefathers, Dasharatha donated four lakhs of the cows and gold to the poor and money to the brahmans. Then the king, Dasharatha shone very brightly. While he was doing this, the father-in-law of Bharatha came to Mithila. He greeted the king, Dasharatha later.

The father-in-law of Bharatha told that his father had conveyed his regards to Dasharatha. And he wanted to see the prince, Bharatha. So that made him come to Mithila. He said that he had gone to Ayodhya and there he had known about the marriages in Mithila. Then Dasharatha greeted him back. Later they went to the place where Srirama and Laxmana were hosted and all of them stayed there happily. Next morning, accompanying Vishwamitra and Vashishta, Dasharatha went to the yagna's spot.

Srirama along with his three brothers performed pre-marriage rituals. Vishwamitra and Vashista along Dasharatha asked Janaka for a bride as it was a part of tradition. Then Janaka said that they were already waiting at the marriage platform. The two brides were shining like red fire. Then the king Dasaratha took his sons to the platform. They went up to the platform. The platform was decorated with scandal flowers.

Gems in golden bowls, peculiar pots, droop sticks and with all the traditional items, the platform was exquisitely decorated. Vishwamitra and Vashista were chanting mantras and performing yagna. Meanwhile Sita was taken by maids and made her sit before Srirama. Then Janaka told Srirama, "Rama! Receive my daughter as your wife. Hold her hand be with her for the lifetime in every situation" Then the musicians played the music and Vishwamitra and Vashista started marital mantras. And the rain of flowers showered.

The following day Vishwamitra was bidden farewell by everyone over there. Later the king, Dasharatha said that they also would start for Ayodhya. Kujadwaja and Janaka presented one lakh of cows, silk clothes, elephants, horses, chariots, jewellery to the four young princes. While the four couples were proceeding to Ayodhya, the birds in Mithila sang terribly and the animals roamed aimlessly.

Then Dasharatha asked Vashista what the reason behind it. He also questioned whether it might happen to them. The king, Dasharatha was doubtful in That regard. He felt that it was augury. Then Vashista told the king that the terrible singing of the birds and roaming of the animals were the signs of something terrible happening. Meanwhile the sudden gale made the trees fall onto the ground. And the sun was covered with black clouds. Then it became dark and they didn't know which way to follow. The army was covered with plenty of dust. Their journey was stopped because of the unexpected disturbance.

Then Parusharama, who defeated many kings, suddenly appeared before them. He wore his axe and was looking ferociously. He was almost looking like lord Shiva. And he also brought a bow which looked like lightning. They thought Parusharama started slaughtering the kings. They had a conversation with him peacefully so that he would not get angry.

Then Parusharama came forward and started speaking with the prince, Srirama this way, "Srirama! I came to know that you had braced the bow of Shiva. I can appreciate that. I felt surprised on hearing that. Now I brought another bow to you. This is the most frightful bow of mine. Now prove your strength by bracing this bow. If you can I can fight with you"

On hearing the words of Parashurama, the king, Dasharatha

was in grief. Then he spoke with Parashurama, "Parashurama! You have stopped fighting with the kings and become appeased. Please do not show your strength before the young princes. Please leave my son. You were born in the dynasty of Bhargava and gave up using weapons. You have the greatness of donating the mother earth to Kashyapa"

But Parusharama did not listen to the words of the king and started walking towards Srirama. He said that the two greatest bows were the bow of Shiva and the bow of Vaishnava. One had already been braced by him. He also said that the bow of Vaishnava was more powerful than the bow of Shiva. It had the history of defeating the bow of Shiva. Then Shiva had stopped. Then all the gods stopped the fight between Lord Vishnu and Shiva.

Later the bow of Vaishnava was given to Devaratha and next to Ruchika and later to my father and my father gave it to me, said Parusharama. My father who abnegated the bow, was killed by Kaartha Veeryarjun. Then I killed him with vengeance. I, who was on meditation on the hill of the mountain of Mahendra, came here to give it to Srirama. Now he has to brace it. Then I will fight with him, said Parusharama.

On hearing the words of Parashurama, Srirama told him that he had listened about the greatness of him. You had settled the debt of your father but why do you suspect my ability and the brightness in me. Then Srirama took the bow of Vaishnava from the hands of Parusharama. Since you are Brahman, the bow would not be in your hands. Because, it kills the lives of the people, I am not going to see that you use this. Srirama said that he was going to break so that the world would be saved from it. Later Srirama had braced the bow of Vaishnava.

Then Parsharama replied to Srirama, "I had donated the mother earth to Kashyapa many years ago. Then Kashyapa, my teacher told me not to roam on the earth at night. Since it was becoming dark, I had to go back to the mountain of Mahendra.

Parusharama told to destroy the bow without any delay. I can sense that you are a replica of lord Vishnu. Everything will be good and I do not feel shy to be defeated by you. If you break the bow, I can go to the mountain. Suddenly all the directions shone brightly. All the gods appreciated Srirama from heaven. Then Parusharama adored Srirama and went in the south direction.

After Parusharama had gone, Sriram gave the bow to the god of rain. Later Sriram spoke with his father in this way, "Parusharama went and we can start for Ayodhya" Then Dasharatha came to him and embraced. He told that he had felt like his son was born again because no one till then escaped from Parashurama, except Srirama. Later he ordered the army to go to Ayodhya as fast as they could. The people of Ayodhya were waiting for the four couples holding flower garlands. They decorated the streets of Ayodhya and they arranged music to welcome them. When the four couples entered the city, the people lauded Srirama and the others. Later Dasharatha and newly married couples went into the palace which was like the mountain Himalaya.

Kausalya, Sumitra and Kaikeyi welcomed Sita, Urmila, Mandavi and Shrutha Kirthi. Then the princesses were allowed to spend with their husbands privately in their rooms that night. Later a few days Dasharatha spent with his sons and daughters-in-law happily. Dasharatha informed Bharatha and Shatrughna that their uncle, Yudhajith, came and was waiting for them in their mother's room. They went to their mother.

Yudhajith took his sons-in-law to his country on the request of his father. Kaikeyi felt very happy for her sons as they went to see her father. Later Srirama and Laxmana took care of Dasharatha and helped him in the administration. They started slowly learning everything from their father and the people of Ayodhya were also very happy with their rule.

The people especially liked the qualities of Srirama. They knew that he would stand on the truth and righteousness. Srirama and Sita were also very happy for a few seasons. Even Sita won the hearts of everyone in Ayodhya. The people treated Srirama as lord Vishnu and Sita as Laxmi. Thus everyone in Ayodhya was very happy.

CHAPTER TWO

Ayodhyakanda

Bharatha was going to his uncle's house along with his brother, Shathrugna. There they were affectionately looked after by his maternal uncle. After a few days, they suddenly recollected their father, Dasharatha. But their father was very far from the place. Even Dasharatha felt the same as Bharatha and Shatrughna. The king, Dasharatha had four sons and all of them were virtuous. Of the four, Srirama was the eldest and he was very dear to his father.

Srirama was a person who maintained stoicism. He never worries or feels happy with the incidents in his life. He always maintains his thoughts secretly. He has honest followers and friends. He is ready to give up anything which benefits others with his sacrifice. He is always punctual. He respects the elders. He doesn't absorb the evil and stable minded. He doesn't have the qualities of laziness, indiscipline and despair. He agrees if he commits the mistakes. He has wisdom in everything. He doesn't forget the help of others. He has the power of discretion and is able to differentiate between good and bad. He has the quality of righteousness. He is skillful at war and he doesn't respond if anyone is angry with him. He is not jealous and conquered the anger. He has no vanity and is loyal to everyone.

Srirama is the most handsome man and nobody could beat him at war. He is equal to his father, Dasharatha in all aspects. He maintains peace and speaks in a soft manner with everyone. If anyone talks to him in a rude manner, he will not reciprocate. He remembers the person who helped and forgets who hindered his growth. He is revered and loved by the people. He has the capacity to resist all the senses.

Since he has all the qualities, Dasharatha thought to make him the king of Ayodhya after discussing with his ministers. Dasharatha invited all the kings of surrounding provinces to discuss it. But he did not invite the kings of Kekaya and Janaka. Many kings were present in the excitement. After felicitating all of the kings, Dasharatha started the discussion of making Srirama the king of Ayodhya.

The king, Dasharatha spoke solemnly in the meeting about Srirama's incarnation. He told them about his kingdom and its greatness. He also told them how his ancestors ruled it wisely. The king said that he had become fragile ruling the country for thousands of years. "Now I need peace of mind and rest in my body," he said. With the consent of the people, priests and everyone in the kingdom, I decided to make Srirama as the king of Ayodhya.

He said, "My son has all the qualities to become a king. He is equal to lord Indra in ruling. He become the youngest king in this country. He is superior to all of his younger brothers in everything. If I make him king, I will be free from the stress and I will live the rest of my life with the rest. This is what I have been thinking past few days.

If you allow, I will make him the king. This is my wish so think about this" On hearing the words of the king, Dasharatha, all the king's present over there felt very happy with his wise decision. Even the nature thrilled with the king's decision. As a result of that, it rained and peacocks danced. The crowd in the hall jeered with the decision.

All of them in the hall said to the king, Dasharatha in this way, "Oh my dear king, since you became very old, making Srirama the king of Ayodhya is also our wish. We agree with your decision. We want to see Srirama as the king of Ayodhya. And we want to see him praised by the people"

With the reply of kings and priests, Dasharatha felt joyous. The king, Dasharatha asked them, "Why would they want to see Srirama as the king of this country while I was ruling the country?" Then they replied that Srirama was the prince with multiple good qualities. He was truthful and honest. They said that Srirama was the best prince of all Ikshvaku kings. He always greets the people and knows their welfare by roaming on the horse. They told me that they had never seen that kind of prince before. When the people were in the struggle, he felt as if it was his struggle. It is better to make him the king for the country's welfare. And he has all the qualities to become a king, they said.

Finally everyone in the hall kept the ball in Dasharatha's about incarnation of Srirama. Later the king, Dasharatha speaks to his elder son, Srirama. He told Srirama, "Everyone in the country is longing to make you king. Since it is the month of Chaitra, the sacred month, I decided to make your incarnation as the king of the country" Later he called Vashista and Vamana to make preparations for the incarnation. He told them to arrange gold, clothes, flower garlands, honey, chariot, puffed rice, elephants, umbrella, golden pots, golden horns, skin of a tiger. He ordered them to arrange them at the yagya mandap.

The doors and gates of the palace were decorated with scandal paste, flower garlands and lightened with dhoop sticks. About one lakh brahmans were arranged and nutritious food was prepared for them. Dasharatha told them to arrange the things to felicitate the brahmans after the incarnation. The flags were tied along the streets in Ayodhya. Vashishtha and Vamana said that they would arrange all of the things which were told by Dasharatha.

Later Dasharatha ordered his minister, Sumantra to bring Srirama before him and he brought him to the palace in the chariot later. When Srirama was coming, all the kings and gods applauded him. While everyone was seated on their respective thrones, all the kings saw Srirama. Dasharatha felt very happy for his son who was handsome like the moon. He was not satisfied to see him at once so he looked at his son many times. The more he sees him, the more he gets happiness. Sumantra got Srirama down from the chariot and led him into the palace.

Srirama later climbed onto the platform where his father was seated which was like Kailasa of Lord Shiva. Srirama saw his father and prostrated to him. Then Dasharatha hugged his son with utmost pleasure. Then he told his son to be seated on the decorated throne. When he sat on the throne, he shone like the morning sun. The hall looked like a constellation as everyone was looking awesome. Dasharatha was on cloud nine looking at his son who was adored by everyone in the hall. Dasharatha, who was like

Kashyapa, spoke to his son in this way.

Srirama you are my dearest son. You are revered by everyone in the country with your good qualities. So you take my throne as it is the time of the star of pushyami. Though you are eligible for the throne, I once again tell you to accept the princehood. After becoming the prince, you should conquer all of your senses and become dear to everyone. First you should win the hearts of the ministers then the people. If you win the hearts of the people, you will be adored by them forever.

So my dear son! I am not electing as the prince. You are electing yourself as the prince with your multiple good qualities. Later Kausalya was informed about the incarnation as Srirama requested them to bring his mother in. Kausalya, who was the gem among all the women, came there. She was also very happy to see her son becoming the prince. She presented gold and cows to the poor with happiness. So everyone was joyous with the event.

After the people had left the palace, Dasharatha spoke with his ministers that the next day would be an auspicious day to make Srirama the prince. Later he went into their house. There he again called the minister to bring Srirama to his room. The minister went to Srirama's room and told him that his father wanted to see him again. Srirama asked why his father again wanted to see him. The minister said, "I have no idea Srirama '' Then Srirama started for his father's room immediately. Dasharatha saw his son and invited him into his room. Then Srirama saluted his father with his two hands. Dasharatha stood and hugged his son. Later he told his son this.

My dear son! I have become old and feeble. I have experienced everything in my life. And I performed plenty of yagnas in my life. God blessed me with the wonderful sons. I have learnt many things. So my life becomes full when I do your incarnation. Listen to my instructions. Everyone in the country wanted to see you as the king. So first I will make you as the prince then automatically you will become the king after my demise. I had nightmares. In the dream I saw comets and asteroids. These convey that something terrible is going to happen. So I may die at any moment. It is imperative you become the prince. Tomorrow on the star of Pushyami, the auspicious moment I will do your incarnation. My heart is beating so fast. So before you become the prince you have to be on fast without eating anything and have to sleep on the floor instead of on the luxurious bed.

There are a lot of well wishers who support you in the kingdom. If we are late, we might confront obstacles. We don't wait for Bharatha. During his absence we should do the incarnation. Do not worry about him, he will obey his father's orders. He can understand the situation well. But we don't believe in the people who will change at what time. Dasharatha gave full instructions to his son and told him to leave and do so accordingly.

Then Srirama prostrated to his father and went to his mother's room to take her blessings. When he went there Kausalya was performing Laxmi puja. The ministers were already present knowing that Srirama was coming there. Even Sita was there along with Kausalya knowing her husband would be incarnated. She was doing puja for her son so she did not notice Srirama's presence.

When she opened her eyes, he went to his mother and took her blessings. Srirama said to his mother, "My dear mother, father has ordered me to get ready for the incarnation. He wanted to see me as the prince. So tonight my wife, Sita, has to go fast. Tomorrow we will perform the rituals for the incarnation. On hearing the words of her son, Kausalya felt very happy and she'd tears of joy.

Kausalya said, "My dear son! I always bless my sons. I pray to god that you would live a longer life with abundant health and wealth. After a long time I am very happy. The news thrilled my heart. I knew that you would become a great person as you were born on the auspicious star. That is why you were adored by everyone along with your father. Now I am soothed by your words. I bless you that you will stand your dynasty to the heights.

Later Srirama smiled at his mother and turned to Laxmana, who was his friend and brother. He said to Laxmana, "Apart from me, you also rule the country as if you were my second soul. I do not crave wealth. So experience the wealth and I look after the people" next Rama and Laxmana took the blessings of their mothers and went to their room. Sita accompanied Srirama.

The king, Dasharatha called the priest to speak about the incarnation of Srirama. He told the priest, Vashishtha, to prepare Srirama on the fast. Then Vashishtha went to Srirama's room. Srirama, who saw his teacher, stood and welcomed him into his room. Then Vashishtha told him that Dasharatha was very happy for him as he was going to rule the country. So apart from Srirama, his wife, Sita had also to be on fast before Srirama's incarnation in the morning.

After Srirama had adored him, Vashishtha left the place. Srirama sent him an honour. Srirama felt very happy because his teacher came and instructed him. When Vashishtha went out, he was astonished to see a huge crowd outside. And they started doing the celebrations by singing and dancing.

All the people in Ayodya were waiting for the day break. They were eagerly waiting to see the grand ceremony. Vashishtha slowly went out from the crowd and reached the palace with much difficulty. He met Dasharatha as if Jupiter met lord Indra. On seeing Vashishtha, Dasharatha woke up from his bed and enquired if he had done accordingly. He said that he had given the instructions to Srirama how to be on fast. Then Dasharatha was joyous and with the permission of Vashishtha and the king's over there, went into the living room. When Dasharatha was going all stood in reverence. The palace looked beautiful with the ladies and decorations. It was shining like the moon in the sky.

After the priest had gone, Srirama took bath and started adoring Vishnu along with his wife, Sita. Later he started pouring the ghee on fire. After the puja had been completed, Srirama and Sita were waiting for dawn. Meanwhile he made Sita to decorate his room for the pastime. When the day broke, Srirama heard the noises of the people from the outside. He again took a bath and wore silk clothes. Then the priests came to his room and made him read Swasti Suktam. The city, Ayodhya became sacred with the melodious mantras of the priest and the music played by the musicians. The people were on cloud nine looking at the couple Srirama and Sita who had just finished their fasting.

Flags were tied, the children were told the stories about Srirama, streets were decorated with scandal flowers, the dhoop sticks were lightened. The people were so eager to see the incarnation. The people gathered in crowds were discussing the event. The king, Dasharatha was appreciated by them for making Srirama their prince. They expected Srirama's rule in advance and hoped that he would rule like Dasharatha. The people knew that he would treat them as if his brother. They witnessed his qualities showing love and affection for his brothers. And they saw his qualities so they were blessed to live long as their king. The news was spread all over the country. The people in groups from all sides started coming to Ayodhya to see the incarnation.

A lady, Mandhara whose birthplace was not known, climbed onto the balcony. Mandhara was a maid of the third wife Dasharatha. She was looking beautiful with her eyes which were like a lotus. She was surprised to look at the joyous people and decorated streets. Immediately she rushed to Kaikeyi who was in her room.

Mandhara asked, "Why were the people of Ayodhya very happy?" She asked her sarcastically whether Kausalya might have given them money. Later she came to the point and told her about the incarnation of Srirama. Then Kaikeyi said that she had already known about the incarnation. Kaikeyi then scolded her why she had remained silent while the dangerous thing was going on. Mandhara told Kaikeyi to awake from the sleep and know what was actually going on.

Mandhara started changing Kaikeyi against Dasharatha's decision of making Srirama a prince. When she provoked, Kaikeyi felt miserable. Though Mandhara knew that Kaikeyi felt jealous, she again asked her whether she was unhappy. Then Kaikeyi was angry. Mandhara's plan had worked out by making Kaikeyi polluted with jealousy on Srirama. She started making her mind filled with jealousy. Dasharatha was harming you by making Srirama as a prince. That is why I came here to be helpful to you.

Mandhara said that Kaikeyi's happiness is her happiness and Kaikeyi's grief is hers. She questioned Kaikeyi why she was unaware of the terrible thing about being a royal queen. She also told her that Dasharatha was harming Kaikeyi and her son secretly. He was giving whole wealth to Kausalya and he was giving nothing to her. He deliberately sent Bharatha far away and did incarnation in his absence. "How do you bear the unbearable?" Mandhra asked

"If Srirama becomes the king, you will be killed. So it is better to stop the incarnation and protect yourself" Mandhara said. On hearing the words of her maid, Kaikeyi's face glowed like the moon. Later she presented Mandhara with a necklace to wake her up. She till now had not shown any difference between Srirama and Bharatha but you told me that I have to stand by my son, Kaikeyi said.

Then Mandhara threw the necklace which had been presented by Kaikeyi. She cursed Kaikeyi while she came to make her realize, Kaikeyi was giving the necklace. Mandhara asked when she knew herself. She explained to Kaikeyi why she was happy for trifling things. This is the time for thinking how to stop the incarnation but not for the celebration. I just show pity on you. If you were a clever lady, would you be happy? The development of a co-sister's son is like death. If Srirama becomes the king, it is harmful to Bharatha. Laxmana always accompanies Srirama and Shathrugna accompanies Bharatha. Since Kausalya was lucky, her son is becoming the prince. Since you are a beggar, your son is becoming a servant to them. You next generations will also become the servants to Srirama's generations.

Then Kaikeyi told why she had been worrying. Srirama is a man of letters and has all the good qualities. He conquered his senses. He is the eldest of all and he is eligible for the princehood. He looks after his brothers affectionately. Kaikeyi questioned why she had been worrying instead of her. After Srirama, Bharatha would rule the country. "Do not worry", Bharatha and Srirama both are equal to me. Srirama loves me as her mother. If Srirama becomes the prince, automatically Bharatha gets the power, Kaikeyi said.

Then Mandhara told Kaikeyi that she had been an idiot and not knowing the truth. Her eyes had been covered by innocence. If Srirama becomes the king, he will become the king. She questioned Kaikeyi how her son would be the king. And there are chances of Laxmana becoming the king as Srirama and Laxmana protect each other. If Srirama becomes the king, he can Bharatha to forest. So send Srirama to the forest before he sends your son. This is the actual thing. I am explaining all this for your benefit, Kaikeyi said.

Kaikeyi continued, once you protested Kausalya, for that she would definitely take revenge through her son. Finally I would suggest you ask Dasharatha to make Bharatha as the prince instead of Srirama and send him to the forest.

After Mandhara had changed her mind, Kaikeyi got very angry at Dasharatha for making Srirama as the prince. She promised that she would send Srirama to the forest and make Bharatha as the prince. Then she asked Mandhara to give good advice in this regard. So Mandhara, who was wicked, told her in this way.

"Once, your husband took you to lord Indra to help him in the war. There your husband fought with rakshasas greatly on behalf of the gods. Then you also helped your husband in the war. Your husband gave two boons to you. He promised in any situation he would fulfill his boons. You told me about this a few years back. You might have forgotten. Now it is the time to use the boons and use them to make your son as the prince and send Srirama to the forest for fourteen years. Then you and your son will be safe from Srirama. So you go to the building of anger wearing ragged clothes. Do not speak to your husband. When he comes to see you, shed tears. Since you are dear to him, he will definitely listen to you"

Then Mandhara felt very happy giving a wonderful suggestion. She was appreciated for her magical knowledge to change minds. She told Mandhara that she would present her a golden garland after her will was fulfilled. Then Kaikeyi said, " First do your task" Then Kaikeyi removed her grandeur clothes and jewellery, wearing the ragged clothes and entered the building in anger.

Kaikeyi had thrown her saries, garlands, and jewellery onto the ground in anger. Dasharatha went to Kaikeyi to inform about the incarnation of Srirama but he did not find her in the room. Someone there told him that she was angry so she had entered the building of the anger.

Dasharatha pondered why Kaikeyi entered the building. He did not get any idea about it. So he went to the building and saw her sulkiness. Dasharatha asked his third wife what made her get angry and why was crying lying on the bed. He asked if she had been suffering from fever then he would call for a doctor to treat the disease. He asked if she wanted something. He consoled her in many ways but she did not stop crying.

After some consolation, Kaikeyi woke up from the bed and said that she was not hurt by anyone. I got angry and entered the building because of not fulfilling my wish that you had promised me to fulfil. Dasharatha was perplexed and asked her what he wanted. She said that she wouldn't believe in him. Then he promised his dearest son Rama. He promised at any cost, he would stand on his word.

Then Kaikeyi recollected his boon which he had promised at the war a few years back. She explained to him how she supported him at the war. Dasharatha recalled the boons and said he is ready to fulfill them now. Kaikeyi, wicked lady told him to stop the incarnation of Srirama and make Bharatha as the prince of the country. And the second boon which Dasharatha has to fulfill is to send Srirama to the dense forest for 14 years. Srirama has to lead his life as a normal person wearing the skin of animals as clothes. She asked that he would fulfill them immediately. She told him to prove his word.

Dasharatha at once fell down on hearing the words of Kaikeyi. He felt as if it was a dream. When he pinched himself, he came to know that it was not a dream. He blamed Kaikeyi for having such wicked desires. He cursed her with abusive words. He asked her what Srirama had done to her, who treated her as if she was his mother. Everyone in the country is longing for Srirama's incarnation. He said that Bharatha was nothing before Srirama's qualities. Take back your desires and I will touch your feet, Dasharatha said.

Once you help but it is not the right way to take back the help. It was okay making the incarnation of Bharatha. But why does Srirama have to go to the dense forest for 14 years and lead a normal life? Does a king worry about giving boons? Doesn't the earth feel sad? Change your mind. Except for the incarnation of Srirama. If you do so I will take poison and die. Thus Dasharatha was crying like anything sitting on the floor.

Even Bharatha was craving for Srirama's incarnation. So change your mind, said Bharatha. He was repeatedly abusing her. I can't live without Rama, he said. But Kaikeyi was not listening to him and she said at any rate that she will be fulfilled. Dasharatha told her to rule the country as a widow. If Srirama goes to the forest, I will die.

Then Kaikeyi spoke out. "Oh my dear king! You are treated as an honest and truthful man on the earth. Will you take back the boons which you gave to me? Dasharatha heard the wicked words and questioned her. Will you be happy while Srirama was facing the struggles in the forest? You will remain as a cunning woman in history. Everyone blames and abuses you. Meanwhile the dusk had fallen. Dasharatha saw the sky and resumed his grief.

He made a final attempt to change the mind of Kaikeyi. But his efforts would end in futile. Dasharatha finally was unconscious with the continuous crying.

Kaikeyi woke up the king, saying it was you who gave me boons and it was you who promised your son Srirama to fulfill my desires. Many in history sacrificed their lives to be on their given word. Why do you cry so much? asked Kaikeyi. Then Dasharatha got his dareness and started speaking up.

Dasharatha promised the god of fire that he was giving up Kaikeyi as his wife and Bharatha as his son. He said that dawn was about to come. Everyone was expecting that the incarnation of Srirama would start. They do not know that happened here. I may die at any moment. You and your son should not participate in my funerals and rituals. Only Srirama would burnt the pyre.

Kaikeyi was angry with Dasharatha for speaking the negative words. Ask your son Srirama to come here and I will send him to the forest. I will make Bharatha the king of the country and we will rule without any enemies. Dasharatha was getting angry but he could do nothing. Then he wanted to see his dear son Srirama.

Meanwhile the day broke and the sun rose. At the auspicious time, Vashishtha entered the palace to participate in the incarnation. He was very happy to see the people who decorated the streets. When he entered the hall, it was overcrowded. And the horse was also decorated.

Sumantra, the minister welcomed Vashishtha and Vashishtha told him to inform Dasharatha about his arrival.

Vashishtha said that everything was ready and ask the king to come to start the ceremony. Sumantra went to Dasharatha and told the same. Then the king, Dasharatha spoke in a feeble voice. Sumantra enquired what had happened to him and what made him speak like that. But he didn't utter a single word. Then Kaikeyi interfered and told the minister to bring Srirama there. Sumantra was perplexed about the situation. He thought how he would follow the instruction of Kaikeyi while the king remained silent. Then the king interfered and told Kaikeyi the same as Kaikeyi. Then Sumantra obeyed the king's order and started for Srirama's room.

When Sumantra went there, Srirama was in the crowd who was being made up for the incarnation. They were discussing the sudden disappearance of Dasharatha. Then Sumantra told them that the king had ordered me to bring Srirama to his room. Then Srirama woke up from the chair and asked him what had happened.

Then Sumantra told Srirama that the king and Kaikeyi wanted to see him. Srirama did not understand why they wanted to see him at this time. He immediately informed his wife, Sita, about the news. Then Sita told him to go to his father. She told him it might be urgent otherwise the minister would not come at this time. Laxmana, his brother was by his side at that time. Laxmana told Srirama that he would accompany him to see their father and Kaikeyi.

So Srirama told Sita that he would take Laxmana. Sita said, "Okay". Srirama and Laxmana bid farewell from there and started to meet their father. The people over there were dumbfounded why they were going at this time. They thought Srirama would take the blessings of his father. In fact the king and Kaikeyi had to come there but they did not understand the king's intention. The suspect fell upon the people. After some time they reached the place where Dasharatha and Kaikeyi were waiting for them.

Srirama was surprised to see his father who was sitting sadly in the chair. He touched the feet of Dasharatha and Kaikeyi. He later asked his father what made him sad. Srirama had never noticed his father crying. This was the first time he was seeing him gloomy. He did not know what had happened to his father. He was terrified of his father's condition. When he asked about his condition, there was no response from his father. So he enquired Kaikeyi what plight had come to his father.

Srirama asked Kaikeyi whether he had committed a mistake. Srirama said to Kaikeyi, "I think he is afraid of you. Something was haunting my father. He was unable to convey it. At least tell me what was in his mind"

Then Kaikeyi told everything what had happened. She told about the boons which the king had given at the war. And she told her desire to make Bharatha as the prince and send him to the forest for 14 years. She told Srirama that she was utilizing her boons now.

On hearing the words of Kaikeyi, he felt surprised and worried. And within a few seconds he came to a normal position. He told Kaikeyi, "If my father orders me to jump into the fire, I will not hesitate. If he orders me to drink poison, I will obey. I am the father's son. I will do whatever he says."

Then Kaikeyi told him to drop from the incarnation ceremony and make Bharatha as the prince and go to forest for 14 years and lead a very normal life there. She told me that she was doing this because of the boons she got from her father. So I asked your father to make my son as the prince and send you to the forest. In the forest you have to lead a very normal life wearing fabric clothes and the skins of animals. This is the thing he wanted to convey to you but he couldn't. Thus Kaikeyi told Srirama boldly. But Srirama did not tremble and react to her words. He took it so positively and behaved as if nothing had happened.

Later Srirama agreed to go to the forest and was ready to make Bharatha as the prince. And he also agreed to wear the fabric clothes. So he was not hesitating for anything. He didn't worry about him. But one thing was haunting him like anything. It was about Sita who married him just a few months back. He would send his people to take back Bharatha to make him prince. But how he would do injustice to his wife, Sita. He was ready to go to the forest alone to prove his father's word. He was not interested in making his father down. He also told his father not to worry about him. He said that it was a very simple thing for him.

On hearing the words of Srirama, Kaikeyi was very happy as her son was going to become prince. She said to Srirama to start in the forest without any delay. She was making preparations to bring Bharatha from his uncle's house to make the prince and later the king.

Dasharatha who heard the words of Kaikeyi felt miserable. He thought how he would live without Rama. And later fainted thinking about Srirama. Later Srirama woke up his father and told him not to worry about him. Srirama told

Kaikeyi that he had no desire for wealth. I live my life in an honest and righteous way. Even though I was ready to go to the forest without my father's order. I will go and live there for fourteen years. First I have to inform my mother and wife about this. I have to take their consent of them.

Dasharatha was crying listening to Srirama's words. He felt how great his son was. Later Srirama took the blessings of his father and Kaikeyi and started to meet his mother, Kausalya. Laxmana who watched all this was furious and he was shedding tears. He was very angry with Kaikeyi. Doing nothing, he followed Srirama.

Srirama, who had to become the king, was going to the forest for 14 years. But he was not worried. He was very happy for fulfilling his father's boons which he had given to Kaikeyi. Meanwhile he reached the palace of his mother. And he went to his mother. Kausalya was surprised to see her son at that time. She wanted to know what had happened. When she looked at Laxmana, he remained silent.

Srirama finally told his mother about the boons his father had given to Kaikeyi and Kaikeyi's desires. When Kausalya heard that, she fainted at once. Later Srirama and Laxmana woke her up and consoled. Kausalya could not stop her grief as her son who wanted to become a prince and was going to forest. Srirama told her that he would fulfil his father's promises.

Kausalya told him if he was not born to her, he would not face such problems. She said that he didn't get happiness till now. While he was about to experience the wealth and luxury, he had to go to the forest. She explained that no mother would experience this kind of pain. If Srirama goes to the forest, I will die, Kausalya said. She also stated all her pujas which she performed for her son would become futile.

Sita, his wife, was crying looking at her husband's plight. She had also been very happy to marry such a wonderful husband. And she expected that he would become king. She never guessed these incidents. Her sadness was not shown like her husband. Thus she also was called the best wife. She proved that a wife should stand by her husband's good deeds.

On seeing the grief of Kausalya, Laxamana was furious. He felt that this was because of wicked, Kaikeyi. He said that he did not like his brother going to the forest. He blamed his old father for listening to his third wife's orders. He called his father the lust king. He opined why his brother would go to the forest. He questioned whether Rama committed any mistakes. He stated that there were no people to find fault with Rama. His brother was equal to god. How cruel his father and his third wife were to send him to the forest.

Laxmana said that no one could do anything as he was by his brother's side. If he goes to the forest, I will kill all the people of Ayodhya and make it like a desert. The people who speak for Bharatha will be punished by bow. I even do not hesitate to kill my father and his third wife. He darely blame his father and compared him to a straw man of straw. If Srirama goes, his father will not rule his kingdom properly. The kingdom would become the country of anarchy.

On seeing the rage of Laxmana, Kausalya spoke with Rama. Did you listen to your brother, Laxmana? So you don't have to become a scapegoat. Follow your heart. Don't listen to the words of Kaikeyi forcefully. Just follow righteousness. You don't have to become a king but be in the palace and serve your father and mother. Even Kasyapa did like that and joined the heaven choir. I don't like you going to the forest so make your mother happy. It is better to eat on grass than to live in a palace. If you leave me, I will die.

Srirama replied to his mother that he had no dare to do like that. He said that he would obey his father's orders. He frankly said that he would do anything that his father ordered him to do. I even do not hesitate to kill the sacred cow at the order of his father. The sons of Sagara died while digging the earth for the horse. Parusharama killed his mother. The greatest people did follow the orders of their fathers. The people who followed the words of their fathers, became the greatest than ever. Thus he consoled his brother, Laxmana.

Srirama continued speaking with Laxmana. I know your mentality Laxmana. And I know what my mother is. Both of you are thinking about me and about my welfare. But I am following the righteousness which is to follow my father's orders. You are right in your ways in the same way I am. So you have to give up the thought process of Kshathriya and follow the tradition of righteousness. Finally Srirama requested his brother and mother to permit him to go to the forest. I promise on my life if you disobey my will. With that word he stopped everyone's objections. He also said that everyone has to accept his father's order.

Unable to speak out anything, Kausalya said that she was not bearing he going to forest. She said that she would die if he left her. But Srirama did not accept his mother's will. And he was ready to go to the forest.

Later Srirama tried to console his brother, Laxmana who was very much angry about the recent happenings. Srirama said, "Give proclamation to the public that there was no incarnation. And he suggested not to behave in a way that his mother is getting hurt. He said that he would not bear the unhappiness of his mother. My father was worried very much about me and I would not make him sad anymore. Immediately I have to wear the fabric clothes and start for the forest.

Srirama opined that this was the god's will. We should not be daring enough to fight with the god. So I do not worry about my incarnation being called off. You also cancel your incarnation. We should not worry about the loss of wealth. Sometimes deeds bring us fortune. So going to the forest may bring us happiness. We should not blame Kaikeyi. It may be the god's will and he wanted us to go to the forest for some reasons. Even our father is part of God's will. So we should act according to the god.

When Srirama consoled, Laxmana who was not convinced with his brother's soothing, was sulky with anger. Laxmana said, "I can't tolerate these happenings. How are you bearing these untoward situations? How do you encourage evil things? How do you fulfill the desires of the enemies? The man who was timid talks about the god. The dare people do not bear these evil things. If I dare, I will even fight with god. Then you will come to know my strength.

The people who asked you to go to the forest, they will have to visit. I will give a proclamation that the incarnation would resume without any disturbances. I will protect you and our kingdom. I will encounter whole people who oppose you. My bow is not a jewellery for me. The work of the bow is to kill the enemies. I will give you the arrow of the north-west so that it will kill everyone. Just permit me to use it. In this way Laxmana requested his brother, Srirama.

At last Kausalya agreed with Srirama on a condition. She said in this way, "You are a lucky son to your father as you are striving to stand your father's name in the history. But your brothers here are leading a luxurious life, how would you live on eating fruits and stems in the forest. She again questioned him whether he had dared enough to go to the forest. She sobbed, ``Does a cow leave its calf?" Then Srirama replied to his mother in this way.

My father was being cheated by his third. While he was worrying about me, it was not fine with you also worrying. If you accompany me, who would take care of him? My father is an honest and truthful man. Srirama reminded his mother that it was the duty of her to take care of his father at this age. So please do service to him. After fourteen years of forest life, I will come back and listen to your words.

After listening to her son's words, Kausalya felt very proud for giving birth to such a son who has noble qualities. And she said that she would not live with her Co sisters. One of them was a wicked lady. So please take me to the forest along with you otherwise you stay back in the palace, Kausalya said.

Then Srirama told, "Husband is the god to wife. It is your duty to take care of him. Bharatha is also a very nice person unlike his mother. He will take care of you until I return. So be patience till then"

Srirama continued, please do not interrupt my decision. You will join heaven if you serve your husband. And you will become a sacred lady. Then she understood why her son wanted to go to the forest. Finally she said, "Okay " But she gave some instructions on how to live in a forest and be safe from the dangerous animals. Srirama said that he would come back and make her happy later. Meanwhile she would be safe looking after her husband.

Finally Kausalya stopped crying and was appeased with the words of her son, Srirama. So she agreed to let her son go to the forest. I couldn't prevent your sacred thoughts. She said, "Go and come back safely. Be careful while you are roaming in the forest. The righteousness will protect since you chose its path. The gods also stand by your side in the forest. You will live long and forcefully since you always listen to your parents' words." Later she called Brahmans and asked them to do puja in the name of her son. After the puja had been completed, Srirama spoke to his mother in this way.

Kausalya craved for Srirama's happiness. She said, "You will live like lord, Indra " Later she tied a band to his hand and that will protect him during his journey in the forest. And it will also prevent him from the deadliest diseases. She wanted to see him again as the king of Ayodhya after his forest life. The gods whom I adored, will protect you. She finally embraced him and sent him to Sita's room.

Srirama later took the blessings of his mother and went to Sita. Sita, who was waiting for him at their room in the palace, was surprised to look at her husband. Srirama bent his head down with grief on seeing his wife. Sita was unable to look at her husband in that condition so she broke into tears. And she questioned him why he had come here while the auspicious time was approaching and why his face was not shining.

Then Rama told his wife that his father was sending him to the forest because he gave two boons to his third wife. And now she wanted to utilize them by making her son, Bharatha prince and sending me to forest. She craved that I should stay in the forest for fourteen years. So I agreed to abnegate the princehood and am ready to go to the forest. So you also support Bharatha in administration. Do not get disheartened.

"As my father was sending me, I decided to go. Hereafter stop fasting and Vratas. Take care of your health and look after my mother. Respect everyone and treat everyone equally. You shouldn't come with me as Kaikeyi craved that I only should go to the forest", said Rama.

Then Sita got angry on his father. She questioned him why his father was sending him to the forest. I thought that you would become king and rule the country, looking after me and your parents. But why this sudden turmoil? I should not bear the news, Sita said.

Srirama tried to convince her. But Sita did not calm down. After long soothing, she said that she would also accompany him to the forest. Srirama was surprised to hear this and he protested. But she is convinced that the husband's duty has to be fulfilled by the wife also. Wife has to accompany in need and deed. Since I am your wife, the punishment will be automatically applicable to me. If you accompany me, I will clear the thorn's path so that your journey wouldn't get disturbed. For my wife, accompanying him is a great thing. I do not live here alone. It is better to die rather than staying alone. I will live in the forest with austerity.

Srirama did not agree with Sita. He said that she would not live on eating fruits and stems in the forest. It will be too difficult to lead the life in the forest. The cruel animals may encounter. But Sita did not listen to him. She pleaded with him to take her to the forest along with him.

By listening to her husband, Sita cried and said in this way. The hurdles in the forest will become dear in accompanying you. She said she liked the animals. If she comes with him she can see plenty of beautiful animals in the forest. She said that she already knew her future. When I was in Mithila, a Brahman told me that I have yoga while staying in the forest. Now I can understand that. Everyone says that following husbands is our righteousness.

Then Srirama agreed to take Sita with him to the forest. Sita's intensity to go with her husband made Srirama agree. She said many stories about the sacred wives who had accompanied their husbands in their hurdles. She said she would die if he did not take her. Them Srirama said, "Okay"

Laxmana, who was watching the argument between Sita and Rama, prostrated to his brother. He said if they both go to the forest, I will not leave here. Please take me My brother. He pleaded with Srirama. But Srirama even tried to convince him as he convinced Sita.

"If both of you come with me, who will look after my mother?" Srirama asked. Our father will be isolated if you come with me. Kaikeyi won't treat him properly. Then Laxmana said everything will be looked after by Bharatha. But I won't be here without coming with you. No one can do harm to our mother and father. Even Kaikeyi won't look after them, our mothers have thousands of acres of land. They will live with the income they get from those lands. So accept me as your guard. It is the duty of me to take care of <u>you in</u> the forest.

Then Srirama agreed to take Laxmana also with him. Later he ordered Laxmana to take two bows and the other material from Dasharatha. After some time he went and came with them. Later Srirama said that he wanted to donate his and his wife's gold ornaments to brahmans. So Laxmana went to take Suyagna who was the son of Vashishtha. After donating them, we will start for the forest, said Srirama.

Later Laxmana goes to Suyagya's house to bring him to the palace. Laxmana tells everything what his brother, Srirama wanted to do. Then Suyagna comes to the palace. Srirama and Sita take blessings from him as soon as he comes. Srirama and Sita remove all the jewellery and give them to Suyagna.

Later Srirama told Laxmana to bring all the money which they had saved. After Laxmana had brought it, they donated it to the old brahmans in the city. Then one of the brahmans named Thrijata got angry with Srirama. He felt that Srirama had pride since he was a prince. To show off he was doing all this. Trijata goes to Srirama and questions him if he had dared enough to donate money to him. Then Srirama tells him that he was going to the forest and because of that he was donating the money. Money is to fulfil minimum needs but it doesn't increase the span of life. Later Thrijata understands everything and goes back happily, taking the thousands of cows and the money.

Later Srirama, Sita and Laxmana go to Dasharatha to ask him to bid farewell to them. Dasharatha feels very proud of his son. He knew that his son had stolen the hearts of the people of the country. That is why he is revered everywhere. Dasharatha tried to convince him finally that he had not to go to the forest. But Srirama does not listen to him. Everyone cries over there with Srirama's decision.

Then Dasharatha asks Sumantra to bring his three wives. We all bid Srirama finally. They all come later. Dasharatha tries to speak with Kaikeyi. He tells her if she was in illusion and she asked Srirama to visit the forest. Meanwhile Srirama interfered with their conversation and stated that he was not interested in kingship. He said that he really was interested in visiting the forest. When he said that Dasharatha cried at once and agreed with his decision. He suggested that his son take the blessings of everybody. He did as his father suggested. Finally Dasharatha asked his son to stay with him that night. And next morning he can start in the forest.

On knowing the grief of Dasharatha, Sumantra was very much angry with Kaikeyi. He immediately told her boldly that it was not correct to make the king sad. He states that he did not see this kind of lady anywhere. He requested her not to insult him before the public. You and your son rule the country. We all accompany Srirama to the forest. He burst out with saying, Srirama was equal to one crore of sons. "Why would she behave like this?" He asked.

He continued by questioning her, "How would she be happy keeping all the people sad?" Everyone one is cursing you. Though Sumantra spoke angrily, Kaikeyi did not move and respond. Dasharatha interfered in his words with Kaikeyi and told him to remain silent. Sumantra obeyed the king's order but his heart was gloomy.

Dasharatha later spoke with Srirama. He said that he would give the army and wealth. He should take them to the forest. He opined that Bharatha couldn't rule without money and army. Then people would refuse him. Then Kaikeyi was astounded with the king's plan. She said, "No one would rule the country without an army and money. It was not correct to do that. Then it would not be a punishment to Srirama. It will be a blessing. She many examples of the people who lived in the forest like Sagara"

Then Dasharatha shouted at her and ordered her to stop the nonsense talk. The people over there were shy. They wondered why their king married this kind of lady. The people also pleaded with Kaikeyi not to send the honest Rama to the forest. But she did not listen to them.

Srirama said that he did not require any wealth and army. I have to live in the forest without any luxuries. So he rejected his father's decision to give money to the army. He asked Kaikeyi to bring the fibre clothes which he wore later. Even his wife, Sita and brother, Laxmana also wore them.

The women in the palace cried with the plight of Sita. They

pleaded with Sita not to go with her husband and rule their country since she was Srirama's husband. But she did not listen to them and firmly said that she should go to the forest with him. Though Kaikeyi asked Srirama only to lead forest life, Laxmana and Sita also decided to go with him.

Now Srirama is looking like a young hermit on the fibre clothes. Dasharatha couldn't see him in the dress. After some time Sumantra ordered his soldiers to bring a chariot. They decided to bid them farewell in the chariot till the edge of the forest. The people told Sita and Laxmana to look after Srirama well in the forest. They blessed him that he should complete the forest life successfully and come back to the country. They hoped at least he would rule their country after fourteen years.

Srirama, Sita and Laxmana prostrated to Dasharatha and Kausalya. Laxmana went to his mother, Sumitra and took her blessings. Sumitra told her son to take care of his brother and Sita. She encouraged him a lot and she felt his decision of going with Srirama was right. She proved that she was an inspirational mother. She also told him to treat Srirama as his father and Sita as his mother during their forest life.

Later Sumantra told them that the chariot was waiting for them outside. Later while crying everyone, Srirama, Sita and Laxmana went out and got into the chariot. Sumantra also got into it and started riding it. The people suggested Sumantra to ride slowly so that they can see him for some time. Kausalya's heart broke while her son was going to the forest. She thought, "How great Laxmana and Sita were!" They were following her son to look after him. While the chariot was moving, the cries of the people echoed through the city. All the people stopped their work and came to see Srirama finally. This was the first time in the history of the whole country shedding into tears.

Dasharatha saw the chariot until his eyes could see. After the chariot had disappeared, he fell onto the ground. Then Kaikeyi tried to hold his hand but he told her not to touch him. Later Kausalya held his hand and lifted him. He requested Kausalya to take him with her to her palace. He said that he was not going to stay in his palace. He would not live there without Srirama and Laxmana. So Kausalya took him to her palace.

In the night he called Kausalya and told her to touch him as he couldn't see her. He also informed her that he was not interested in living his life.

Sumitra consoled crying Kausalya who was gloomy with her son's plight. Sumitra told her not to worry about her son. He is a great son who has all the humane qualities. Laxmana and Sita will definitely take care of him. And Srirama is a great warrior No one could harm him as he had great and powerful arrows. Just wait for a few years he will return and rule the country as the king. Definitely he will make you happy with his deeds.

Kausalya's heart pain subsided after Sumitra had consoled her. She felt very proud of such a son being born from her. She later realized that he had gone for his father. He fulfilled his father's promises by punishing himself.

Sumantra and the people send Srirama off till Tamasa river. There they got off from the chariot Sumantra and watered the tired horses. Thus their journey of forest life started from Tamasa river. Srirama suggested to Laxmana and Sita not to worry and told them to be brave till the end of the forest life. He also told them from that day onwards they should take only fruits and stems.

Later Srirama told Sumantra and the people to take rest on the bank of Tamasa river. Meanwhile Laxmana has prepared a bed which was made of leaves for Srirama and Sita. Later they slept on it that night. Laxmana did not sleep that night. He was acting as the guard for the whole night.

In the early hours Srirama and Sita woke. But the people were still sleeping. Srirama told his brother to continue their journey. He said if the people wake up, they should come along with us. So it is better to start our journey before they wake up. Laxmana opined that they would be hurt if we did so. But Srirama told them that they had no other way than this. He asked Laxmana to arrange the chariot and Laxmana did so. Before Sumantra and the people woke up, they started their journey into the forest.

After some time the people and Sumantra woke up. They were all dumbfounded to notice the disappearance of Srirama, Laxmana and Sita. They later knew that they went on the chariot into the forest. They all cried in the absence of Rama. They came to a decision that they will search for him anyhow. They started their journey. Since the forest was very thick, they didn't find the way which Rama had gone.

With so much pain in the heart, they started back to Ayodhya. They knew that the people of Ayodhya would curse them for doing so. But they had no other option.

When they came back to Ayodhya, they all were questioned by the people. But they stood like statues doing nothing.

After the people had returned from the forest, they cried with their wives and children telling about Srirama. No one was happy in the country. The business men stopped their trades. The farmers did not go to their fields. There was no sight of the markets. The wealth and offspring did not bring them happiness. Everyone was thinking about the plight of Srirama in the forest. They thought what was he eating? Where was he sleeping? They doubted if Laxmana was taking care of him.

They also discussed how the forest became beautiful during his stint. The river smiled when he took a bath in it. Trees become more beautiful. The animals dance freely welcoming him. And they blamed Kaikeyi for sending him to the forest. They felt very bad how she would rule their country. Thus everyone in the country was sobbing for him.

Meanwhile Srirama, Sita and Laxmana went deeper into the forest. They crossed many villages and they observed everyone was abusing Dasharatha and Kaikeyi. After a few days of their journey, they crossed the border of their country, Kosala. After they came across the river Veda Shruti. Later they travelled to the south, there they came the river Gomathi and the river Sandyika. While traveling, Srirama felt he came too far off from their country and he could see the different world. He questioned himself when he would go back to his river, Sarayu.

After a few days, they reached the river Ganges. It contained the sacred water. He tasted it and appreciated its purity. There was a place called Srungarapuram. It was on the bank of the river Ganges. Srirama told Sumantra to prepare for accommodation. That night they wanted to stay there. Sumantra and Laxmana prepared a bed under the tree called Gaara.

The place was ruled by the king, Guha. Guha comes to know that Srirama had come to their place on their journey. He immediately went to the place with his men. On seeing Srirama, Guha felt very happy. He went to Srirama and hugged him with much devotion. Guha told him to treat his place as Ayodhya. He would not have to feel shy for anything. He was ready to provide anything for their comfort. But Srirama said that he was under the punishment. He wouldn't eat anything except fruits and stems. Srirama requested him to treat as a normal person who saunters in the forest. Srirama asked only to provide food for their horses since the horses were very dear to his father. He would not want to see them with hunger. Guha immediately ordered his men to bring food for the horses.

They did evening puja in the river Ganges. While Srirama took a rest under the tree of Sowmitri, Guha and Laxmana started discussing the events in Ayodhya. That night Apart from Laxmana, Guha also acted as the guard to Srirama.

Guha was impressed by Laxmana's care over his brother. The whole night he was guarding his brother. So Guha asked him to sleep for at least a few hours. You are the prince who had to lead a luxurious life but why did he bear so much pain for his brother. Nothing will happen if he sleeps for some time. While my brother is sleeping on the grass and leaves, how he would sleep, Laxmana said.

Laxmana continued if anything happens to him, the whole country will cry. My family members will die if he is hurt little. So I have to look after him well. Guha broke into tears with Laxmana's words. Guha felt how lucky Srirama is to have a fantastic brother. Guha appreciated Laxmana for his affection for his brother.

Next morning, Srirama told Laxmana, "The sun has risen. I could hear the songs of birds. So it is time for us to cross the river Ganges" Guha, who heard this, called his men and told them to bring a boat for crossing the river. Later his men brought it. Then Guha spoke with Srirama that the boat is ready for sailing.

Srirama appreciated Guha for helping him so much. And they got into the boat later. While Sumantra was about to get into the boat, Srirama told him to go back to Ayodhya. Srirama said that they did not require the chariot. After crossing the river Ganges, we will roam on foot in the forest. Then Sumantra agreed to go back and blessed Srirama to have a safe journey in the forest. Sumantra hoped to see them after fourteen years again. Srirama conveyed his regards to his family members and the people of Ayodhya. And he told Sumantra to instruct Bharatha in his administration.

Srirama opines that if Sumantra goes back to Ayodhya, Kaikeyi can believe that we are in the forest or she would think in a different way. Tell everyone that I am brave enough to roam in the forest. Instruct everyone not to cry for me. After Sumantra had gone back, he asked Guha to bring the milk of the banyan tree. Guha did so. With the milk they tied their hair and wore fibre clothes. Later they sailed on a boat in the river Ganges to cross it. Later Guha and his men bid farewell to them. Guha hoped that Srirama would come back and rule his country. He prayed to god that if that happens he will donate one lakh cows to the brahmans and feed them with a sumptuous meal.

After a few hours of sailing they crossed the other end safely. From there they had to go on a walk. Srirama told his brother to always accompany Sita irrespective of the people's presence or absence. Laxmana obeyed his order. Laxmana was walking ahead and Srirama was behind. The two men were acting as the guards to Sita. As they reached the bank, they encountered four ferocious animals and they killed them later.

Srirama, Laxmana and Sita found a tree and they wanted to rest for some time under it. Srirama told his brother not to worry with the absence of Sumantra. Now onwards we both should take care of Sita while she is sleeping.

At night he told Laxmana that his father may not be sleeping with Kaikeyi's wicked nature and she might be enjoying his absence in Ayodhya. It was okay for us to stay in the forest. But with greed, won't she do harm to our father? Our mothers may be worrying about this. Will she create such a mess for making her son the prince?

So Laxmana! Please go back to Ayodhya and take care of our father and mothers. Sita and I enter the thick forest. But Laxmana replied that his brother should not think like that at that moment. He said that his brother was making him sad with his words. He clearly said that he wouldn't live without him and it was his duty to take care of Sita and him. Later they slept under the banyan tree. Later they started their journey in the thick forest. They were roaming in it as if they were lions.

After a few hours of their journey on a walk, they reached the place called Prayaga where the Ganges and the Yamuna merge. The place was so beautiful. Prayaga was spread with fog. There they found evidence of someone living over there. As they expected, they noticed the ashram of Bharadwaja.

They walked into it and met the hermit, Bharadwaja. They introduced themselves. They told everything about what had happened to them and the reason for visiting the forest. Bharadwaja empathized with them after listening to their story. And he gave them fruits and stems of different varieties. Later Bharadwaja asked them to stay with him. But Srirama refused to stay there because many people come to see them everyday if they stay there.

So Bharadwaja told Srirama to go to a place called the mountain of Chitrakuta. The place is very beautiful and it is isolated from the people. If you stay there, you will enjoy nature. And the mountain is very sacred. If you look at it, everything will be auspicious. Many saints performed their meditation for redemption. That night they spent time in the ashram listening to the stories told by Bharatha.

Next morning they took blessings of Bharadwaja and started for the Mount of Chitrakuta. They reached in the evening. They felt wonderful to look at it. The peacocks are dancing, the elephants are honking, the birds are singing and it was the most beautiful place they had ever seen. Sita liked it very much. So they decided to make a hut and to live there.

They later found another ashram at the mount of Chitrakuta. They entered the ashram and later they came to know that it was Valmiki's. They saluted the hermit, Valmiki and he welcomed them into the ashram. Valmiki felt very happy for their decision to build a hut there. With the permission of Valmiki, Laxmana constructed a hut named Parnasala with the dried wood in the forest. He constructed it with utmost care. That is why it looked so beautiful later.

Srirama seeing Parnasala, he wanted to perform puja with the meat of a deer. So he ordered his brother to kill a deer and bring the meat. So Laxmana went and hunted a deer peeled the skin and brought the meat. Later he grilled it in the fire.

After the meat had been prepared, Srirama performed puja according to rituals and entered Parnasala. They felt very happy seeing the fantastic hut. After so many days Parnashala had brought them happiness. It made them forget the nostalgia of their country.

Meanwhile Sumantra reached Ayodhya. When he entered the city, he was surrounded by so many people and asked about Rama. He said that Srirama was on the bank of the river Ganges. Srirama told him that he would return to Ayodhya. People cried on hearing the words of Sumantra.

Suddenly Sumantra heard the cries of Kausalya, Sumitra and Kaikeyi from the windows of the palace. Sumantra immediately entered the palace and saluted the king, Dasharatha. Sumantra carried the words of Srirama to Dasharatha. Everyone was with solemn faces in their grief.

Dasharatha enquired Sumantra where his sons had gone. And he asked if they were all safe. He said that everyone was safe. They conveyed their regards and told me not to worry about them. Sumantra told them that Srirama, Laxmana and Sita were living with courage. So do not worry about them, said Sumantra.

Ayodhya became like a desert after Srirama had gone to the forest. Since the farmers did not work, the crops did not yield. The traders had no business to do as there were no crops. Even the drought had fallen. As a result of this the trees and the rivers dried. The animals were becoming almost extinct, lacking food to them.

The people were not interested to see the king for his weakness. They called him a man of straw. On knowing the condition of Ayodhya, Dasharatha cried a lot. He asked Sumantra to take him to Srirama. He would not see his country without him. He was crying and crying. He suddenly fell from the bed onto the ground. Kausalya saw her husband's plight and she started crying. She also asked Sumantra to take her to Srirama. No one could console Kausalya. Dasharatha woke up with a sound made by Kausalya. He went to her and embraced. He requested her to stop sobbing. Then Kausalya stopped crying thinking about Dasharatha's condition. Meanwhile the dusk had fallen and the sun had set. It had become completely dark.

Suddenly Dasharatha recalled the anecdote. Once, Dasharatha went for a hunt in the forest. He shot and killed Shravana Kumara thinking that he was to be an animal. His parents were blind. They knew that Dasharatha had killed their lovable son. So they cursed him to live without sons. They exclaimed that he should know the pain of living without a son. He shared the episode with Kausalya. He told her something was happening to his heart. He suddenly closed his eyes in the lap of Kausalya. Sumantra came and checked his pulse. With so much pain, he stated that the king passed away. Kausalya broke into tears at once. His last words were "Srirama would be blessed after fourteen years"

The news was spread in the palace. Sumitra and Kaikeyi rushed to the place. They tried to wake him up but they lately realised that he had passed away and joined the heaven choir. The people in the huge crowd gathered in the palace. They thought something evil had occupied their kingdom. They are unable to digest the journey of Rama to the forest and sudden demise of their king.

Kausalya (crying)questioned Kaikeyi whether she was happy the king died. Kausalya said, "Now lead the luxurious kingdom. No one will question you. I will also die. My son is not even with me to console" Everyone in the country blamed Kaikeyi for her wicked qualities. Whole country was in a mess without Srirama and Dasharatha.

Thus everyone spent their miserable night after the king had been demoted. As the day broke, some of the brahmans flouted Vashista. They said that the country had no king. The people are worrying about the lack of proper rules. Their opinion is that anarchy prevailed in the country after Srirama had gone to forest. And now the king even demises. So they opined it was not good for the country. Even Bharatha was not there. He went to his uncle's country. "Who will look after the kingdom?" They questioned.

Vashishta immediately sent some soldiers to the kingdom of Kekaya to bring Bharatha and Shatrughna from their uncle. They started on horses to the kingdom. Vashishtha told not to reveal that Srirama had gone to forest and about the demise of Dasharatha. They should simply assume that he had some work in Ayodhya.

That night Bharatha had dreamt of nightmares. He dreamt that his father had fallen into the river from the mountain. This made him frightened of his father's health. He doubted if something had happened to his father. His uncle tried many efforts to reduce his fright. But his effort ended in futile.

The next morning to his surprise, soldiers from Ayodhya appeared in Kekaya. They told the king that they should take Bharatha and Shatrughna to Ayodhya immediately. Then the king questioned if anything had happened in the kingdom. But they lied and did not reveal the demise. The king ordered Bharatha and Shatrughna to start for Ayodhya immediately. The king arranged healthy horses for them to go to Ayodhya safely. And the king also sent his ministers to accompany them.

Bharatha had a suspicion of the soldiers who came from his country. He doubted why they were so hasty in taking him to Ayodhya. Though he asked them several times, they replied that nothing had happened. After a few days of their journey crossing many rivers and mountains, they reached Ayodhya in the morning.

As soon as Bharatha had set foot in Ayodhya, he heard some noises. The people were crying. He didn't understand what was happening in Ayodhya. He couldn't identify that it was his country as it turned into like a desert. He had no evidence that his country was prospering. He felt something had happened to his country. He sensed a dream and doubted if it was real.

Bharatha straightaway went into the palace. He did not find his father. So he immediately went to see his mother, Kaikeyi. He asked her where his father was. She (sobbing) said that his father had died. At once he fell onto the ground. He was crying like anything. Kaikeyi made him stand and consoled him. He later enquired how his father had passed away. He questioned if any disease made him want to die. He also asked where his brother, Srirama was. The several questions made Kaikeyi suffocate.

Then Kaikeyi told everything, narrating the sequence of episodes and how Srirama, Laxmana and Sita finally went to the forest. She also said that she was the reason for all the mishaps in the country. She told me everything she had done for her son. She suggested him to be the king of Ayodhya.

After knowing everything, Bharatha broke into tears. His lovable father had died and his truthful brother went to the forest. What he would do with the kingdom. He simply rejected her idea of making him king. And he blamed his mother for her wicked things and plans. He told that she had committed sins. For that there was no penance for it. He felt very shameful to say as she was his mother. In any kingdom the eldest becomes the king. He did not get why she had behaved so. He stated that his mother was to be punished. She was eligible to jump into the fire or go to the forest.

Later Shatrughan and he went to meet Kausalya and Sumitra. He felt very disappointed to see Kausalya's plight. She lost her husband and her son had to visit the forest.

Kausalya pleaded with him to send her to Srirama. She explained that she was not interested in living in Ayodhya. Bharatha replied that there was no interference in his mother's wicked plans. He said that he was not interested in ruling the country without his brother, Srirama. He touched her feet to apologize on behalf of his mother.

He explained to Kausalya how he wasn't eligible to become king. And he explained the consequences of becoming king in dishonest ways. He stated many who became like kings in dishonest ways lost their lives brutally. So he doesn't want to be the one among them.

Vashishta consoled crying Bharatha. He said not to cry and was persuaded that everyone has to die one day. He said, "The dead body has to be cremated. It has been a few days since the king was demoted. The dead were decorated and kept in a coffin which was in the hall. He requested Bharatha to fulfil his responsibility of cremating as a son as Srirama was in the forest. In fact the eldest son had to perform to father. Bharatha next went to see his father for the last time. On seeing the yellow body of his father, Bharatha broke into tears. He questioned his father with more pain why he had done all the mess.

Vashishta interfered and suggested Bharatha to start the process for funerals. Later the priests came to spot and started the rituals according to their dynasty. They performed yagna later with the participation of Bharatha. After it had been completed, the dead body was shifted onto the pyre. The pyre was set up with sandalwood and gold. The place was echoed with cry of the people. While the mantras were chanting and three wives were crying, Bharatha lit the pyre. And all went back to the palace after the cremation.

Bharatha was on limited fast for thirteen days. Shathrugna then became furious and shrieked in the palace. He called Mandhara and slapped for influencing his mother. Bharatha was also angry with Mandhara. Vashishta and others stopped them from hurting Mandhara.

On the fourteenth day they celebrated the king's mourning house. Vashishta told Bharatha, "It was a very sad thing, Dasharatha died after he had sent Srirama and Laxmana to the forest. A country without a king would lead to many problems. The country had already been filled with sadness with frequent episodes. So it is the time you became a king. Accept the kingship and save the country from many hurdles. I will arrange for the incarnation immediately"

But Bharatha rejected the proposal of Vashishta. He said, "In our dynasty, the eldest should become the king. It was not the correct decision to make me as the king. I will call Srirama to the kingdom and I will make him king. Instead of him, I will lead forest life" So he requested Vashishta to prepare the army. He said that he would go to the forest to bring Srirama. Everyone appreciated his wonderful decision. He called the architects to build a road to go to the forest.

From the next onwards, they started to construct the road till the river bank of Ganges. Within a few days they could complete the wonderful road. Vashishta informed Bharatha about the completion of the road. And next day, Bharatha started his journey to the forest in the chariot with his army. Bharatha was going in the chariot saying if Srirama comes, the country will be flourished again. The people cheered at Bharatha for saying so. After a few hours of their journey, they reached the place called Srungarapuram. There Bharatha met Guha who was the friend of Srirama. There they halted their journey and decided to stay on the bank of the river Ganges. Guha thought that Bharatha was trying to kill Srirama. He ordered his men to make them countenance. So his men attacked the army of Bharatha. Then Sumantra stopped them and told Guha that Bharatha was a friend of Srirama. He said that Bharatha was a very honest man. Then Guha invited them to his palace along with the army.

Later Bharatha said to Guha that his desire was noble and that is why he had invited them to his palace. Guha replied, "Adoring Sri Rama is a noble thing" Then Bharatha asked him the way to Bharadwaja's ashram. Guha said, "My followers will lead you to the ashram. I will also come with you. I should protect Rama if you are going to harm him. I should see with my own eyes. If you try to harm Rama, my army will attack on you"

Then Bharatha (smiling) briefly said with Guha, "You shouldn't think that at least in the dream. It is not fine to blame me. My brother is my god and equal to my father. I am going to meet him and bring him back. So please do not think otherwise. I promise you. Don't think about me in a negative way"

Then Guha spoke with Bharatha happily. He said that Bharatha was the most humble and honest brother that he had ever seen in his life. No one would abrogate the kingdom that they have got. But you are a noble person. Your goodness is spread over the world. While Guha was speaking, the sun disappeared. That night Shathrugna and he slept in the palace.

While sleeping, Bharatha thought about how the sequence

of actions made the whole family into trouble. He recalled his father's death and brother's forest life. At any way he would want to set their family and bring back the grandeur to their dynasty.

Later Guha and Bharatha started roaming in the forest to find Bharadwaja's ashram. While they were on the way to the ashram, Guha told Bharatha about Laxmana. He said that Laxmana was a very humble brother. When he asked him to sleep, he refused. He was guarding Rama and Laxmana the whole night. He also told that no other person is as lovable as Rama to him.

Guha opined that Dasharatha was the fortunate father in the world as he gave birth to the four sons who had noble qualities. And Dasharatha brought them up with utmost care. When Guha told the story of his brothers and the problems they faced, Bharatha fainted at once.

Bharatha fell onto the ground in the forest. Guha was frightened by that. Shathrugna (crying) embraced Bharatha sitting on the ground. After some time he came into consciousness and started their journey. At first they crossed the river Ganges in boats. From there they walked to Bharadwaja's ashram.

Bharatha ordered his army to remove their weapons and keep them aside as they had to enter the ashram. Bharatha wore silk clothes and walked into it along with the priests. On seeing Bharatha and his men, Bharadwaja stood and welcomed them into his ashram. They exchanged greetings later. Bharatha then questioned him about his brother, Srirama. Bharadwaja then told Sita, Laxmana and he had stayed in his ashram for a night. The following morning he had gone towards the mount of Chitrakuta.

Bharadwaja requested Bharatha and his army to stay back in the ashram that night. He arranged delicious food for the army. They had the food and spent that night. Bharatha said that it was a memorable night they had never experienced. Cuisines of different varieties were served and after the food, yummy dessert was also served.

The next morning after they had spent happily, they started towards the mount of Chitrakuta. Bharadwaja bid farewell to them. He gave a few instructions on how to reach the mount. Next they climbed onto the horses and started their journey in the auspicious time. The journey was beautiful as they saw many rivers and mountains. They saw the river Mandakini on the way. They found some evidence of Srirama and Laxmana. They thought that they had sauntered.

Bharatha ordered his army to stop at the place. Sumantra and he would only go from there to meet them. Bharatha and Shathrugna took their weapons and walked into the forest.

Srirama was showing the beautiful sceneries to Sita as she was feeling very bore staying only in the hut. Sita told Rama looking at the beautiful places that she did not want to go back to Ayodhya as they were making heart pleasant. She felt awesome looking at the beautiful birds, animals, trees, brooks, lakes, ponds, rivers and the sky.

Srirama told Sita that his forest exile for fourteen years had brought him happiness instead of making him very disappointed. First one was that he could fulfill his father's promise and the second one he could make Bharatha as the prince which Kaikeyi liked the most. And he also could spare some time with his wife looking at beautiful places. He had shown the beauty of the mountains which were in different colours.

After they had crossed the mountains, they came across the beautiful river named Mandakini. The river contained beautiful dunes and there were white swans in large numbers. On looking at them, Sita jumped with joy. On the bank of the river Mandakini, many varieties of fruits and flowers were there. They saw the hermits taking bath in the river.

After some they climbed onto the rock and were eating fruits. From a little distance Srirama could notice people were coming towards them. Srirama thought people came for hunting. He informed Laxmana to observe who they were and why they were coming here. Then Laxmana immediately climbed onto the tree and looked at the surroundings. He told Rama that a big army was coming towards them. Rama immediately wore his weapons and got ready to fight with them. When the army came nearer, Laxmana could notice their brother, Bharatha was coming along with the army. He instantly told Rama that it was their brother, Bharatha. Laxmana was furious with Bharatha as he was the reason for their exile for fourteen years. At anyhow, he could kill them and protect Rama. But Rama suggested him not to behave like that. He said that Bharatha was a very nice and humble person.

After some time Bharatha spoke with Shatrughan in this way. Now it is the time, we started searching for Rama, Sita and Laxmana. He ordered his men to search every nook and corner in the forest. I will not be satisfied until and unless I see my brother. Everyone started searching for them. Meanwhile Bharatha noticed smoke coming, when he climbed onto a tree.

Then he climbed down and informed his brother. Later everyone felt very happy. Bharatha and Shathrugna started in the direction where the smoke was coming from. After some time of their walk, they saw the beautiful hut. In front of the hut, they found fabric clothes. Bhartah recalled that it was the same place which Bharadwaja had said about it.

He straightaway went into the hut and his brother, Srirama who was sitting wearing the deer skin. Seeing his brother in that condition, he broke into tears. Crying, he directly went and touched Srirama's feet. Even Shathrugna did the same. They questioned him whether that kind of life was not necessary for him. They begged him to return to their kingdom. Later they went to Laxmana and Sita and asked them the same. They felt sorrowful looking at Sita. The young princess, who had to lead a luxurious life, came to the forest for his brother.

They also requested Laxmana to convince Rama and to see that he would come back to Ayodhya. After some time, Rama asked Bharatha, Shatrughan and Sumantra whether they were fine. Later Rama enquired about his father and mother's health. He doubted if they were not still thinking about them. Then Bharatha with so much pain, he told them that their father was no more. When Rama heard that he immediately was into unconsciousness.

Laxmana was afraid of Rama's unconsciousness. He sprinkled water on him to wake him up. Rama stated that his father had died because of him. For this he felt very shameful. He might have cried continuously for me and that might have caused his death. He was continuously blaming himself. Bharatha intervened and said that he was not the reason for it. The god had given him complete life and after that he joined the heaven choir.

Later Bharatha explained Rama the condition of Ayodhya. He said that the anarchy had prevailed in the country. Apart from it, the drought also had made the country with penurity. So he requested Rama to come back to Ayodhya and to accept the kingship to prevent from all the ailments. He made recall Srirama's qualities and how they make save their country from the danger.

But Srirama did not accept the proposal of Bharatha. Then all the people over there pleaded him to accept the kingship and they asked him to come back to Ayodhya. All the words of them could not convince him. Rama stood on his word. Then Bharatha fell on Rama's feet to accept. Then Rama gave his golden foot wear to him. Rama said that he would come back after fourteen years of exile. Then he will accept the kingship. Till then you rule the kingdom and look after our mothers. He would stand on his word and wouldn't let his father's promise down. I will prove that our father is a very great man and I am a great son who fulfilled my father's promise.

Doing nothing, Bharatha took his foot off and agreed to be the king for fourteen years. He asked to complete the rituals as an elder son he had to perform. Rama agreed to that. The hermits and priests started the ceremony and Rama as an elder son presented the ritual food to his father. And he prayed that his father's soul will be appeased in heaven with the rituals. After that Bharatha and his army went back to Ayodhya. Rama, Laxmana and Sita bid farewell to them.

Bharatha takes the footwear of Srirama to Ayodhya along with his army. The hermits who came along with him to find Rama, went back to their ashrams. On the way to Ayodhya, Bharatha met Bharadwaja and told him what happened in the mount of Chitrakuta. Somehow he could go back to Ayodhya and inform his people that he had met his brother. He told me to put his foot wear on the throne and rule until his forest exile completes. The people reduced their sadness and hoped that he would come after fourteen years and will be their king.

After everyone had gone, Srirama decided not to live in the place as it was being haunted with Bharatha and Shatrughna memories. So he decided to live at another place in the forest. They started going forward in the forest. They reached a place called Athriya's ashram. He welcomed them and gave them accommodation. He treated Rama very well. Athriya's wife Anasuya treated Sita as if she was her daughter. Athriya told them that his wife, Anasuya had done a great penance to take the Ganges to their place.

After knowing her Srirama, Laxmana and Sita respected her. Sita explained to her how she had married Rama. After spending a few days there, they decided to move on. While they were going, Anasuya gave Sita a few jewels as a token of love for her. Sita wore them and thanked her. Rama, Sita and Laxmana again started their journey to find a new place to live in.

CHAPTER THREE

Aranyakanda

After Bharatha and Shathrugna had gone back to Ayodhya, Rama, Laxmana and Sita entered the dreadful forest, named Dandakaranya. After walking for few days in the forest, they found Tapachula Ashram. The ashram was more beautiful than the previous'. They found different kinds of animals, trees and birds which they had never seen before. The ashram was like the house of Brahma. The hermits in it were chanting mantras and it echoed with positive sanctity. When they entered the ashram, the hermits were so happy to see Rama, Laxmana and Sita in their ashram. The hermits saw them for a while without blinking their eyes.

They received the hermits' hospitality with grandeur. Later the hermits felicitated Rama, Laxmana and Sita as they were equal to gods to them. They provided fruits, stems, water and the others to eat. They told Rama that he was a great person who had popularity all over the world. They knew him to be a humble man, who always stands on righteousness and truth. They said that it was their duty to protect him as well as Laxmana and Sita. They stated, he was their king and god irrespective of his place if it was a forest or city.

Rama, Laxmana and Sita spent that night in Tapachula ashram and started their journey in the early morning. On their way, they crossed the mount of Suryodaya. They entered the dense forest which had a lot of tigers and bears. There was no sign of any lakes and rivers in it. The dreadful voices of crickets and birds were heard.

Suddenly they encountered a giant man who was looking like a hill. His eyes were deep and he had a big mouth. His trembling appearance frightened them. He wore the skin of a tiger and wore the skulls as if it was garland. On seeing Rama, Laxmana and Sita, he ran towards them. Sita was afraid of looking at his giant, terrible figure.

He was shouting at Rama, Laxmana and Sita. He asked them who they were. Why were they roaming in the forest with a lady? He told them that he was Viradha. He also said that he was living in the forest hunting the animals and eating their meat. He looked at Sita and admired her beauty. He asked Rama to give her to him. Otherwise he would kill Rama and Laxmana. When Sita heard that she was rattled by his words.

Later Rama told Viradha everything, why they had to roam in the forest along with his wife and brother. Laxmana interfered with their conversation and asked his brother why he had to make conversation with the giant instead of killing him. Laxmana asked permission to kill him with his powerful arrow.

Then Viradha, the giant man interrupted Rama and Laxmana's conversation. He roared at them and asked why they were making a mess while he was speaking. Rama asked him who he was and how dare he speak to them in a rude manner. Then the giant man told that he was the son of Shathahrada. All the rakshasas call me Viradha in this forest. He told that he had done the great penance, for that Lord Brahma appeared and gave me a boon. The boon was that no one would kill me.

So Viradha ordered Rama to leave Sita and went back otherwise he would kill them. When Rama heard that, he raged on the giant. Rama's eyes turned red for speaking so. Then he said to the giant, "You are an evil giant. How dare you speak like that? You are looking for your death. I will definitely kill you in the war" Rama immediately took his arrow from his quiver and shot at the giant. Then the arrow was split into seven and they pierced into his body. With that his body was torn and blood started coming out like a flow. He immediately fell onto the ground.

After some time the giant again woke up from the ground as the arrows hurt him little though the blood poured. When he woke up, the two brothers again started shooting arrows at him. He defended all of the arrows with his shula. He later threw his powerful shula at the brothers. Then Rama defended with his arrows. The arrows broke the shula into two pieces. Then Rama and Laxmana took their swords and pierced into his body. Though he was in pain, he lifted Rama and Laxmana onto his arms.

Then Rama told Laxmana to let him carry us on his shoulders. Sita cried looking at Rama and Laxmana. She pleaded with the giant not to kill them. Without them I will not exist. Tigers may kill me, said Sita. Rama worried looking at Sita. He immediately broke his two arms with his divine strength. With that he again fell onto the ground but he was alive.

Then Rama told Laxmana, "As long as he is on the earth, he will not be killed. So it is better to bury him" Later Laxmana had dug a deep and wide pit. Meanwhile Rama had set his foot on the giant's throat. Then Viradha came to know the power of Rama. Then he realized and said that he couldn't identify his strength. He stated that Rama had the equal strength of Lord Indra.

Then Viradha told his story. He told them that he was killed by Tumbura and cursed by Kubera. Kubera cursed me to live as Rakshasa until you will kill me. Today I was killed and I am very happy today for becoming Gandharva again which was my previous birth. He thanked Rama and Laxmana for ending his curse as Rakshasa. Then Rama kicked on his throat. Simultaneously Rakshasa's life turned into Gandharva. Later he went to paradise. The dead body was buried later.

Rama after killing the giant, hugged Sita and he said to her that the forest was very dangerous. Though it was very tough for us to live in the forest, it was inevitable. After a few hours of journey in the forest, they reached Sarabhanga Maharshi. There they saw a wonder. There was a chariot in the ashram. It was shining like the sun and it was in the sky. It was flying in the air. They wondered how the heavy chariot was flying in the air without touching the ground. The green horses were tethered to it. There they also found a white umbrella. It looked exactly like the moon.

And it was shining with the wonderful flower garlands. There the maids were creating air flow with the handmade fans and the gandharvas were roaming around them. Many hermits were chanting the mantras from Vedas in the sky. Lord Indra was speaking to Sarabangha Maharshi. Rama felt very happy for Lord Indra.

Rama told Laxmana and Sita that they should wait there. He would go towards the place to talk to Lord Indra. Lord Indra saw Rama from a distance and with the permission of Sarabangha Maharshi, Lord Indra allowed Rama into the chariot. Lord spoke to Rama and enquired about their wellness. Indra told Sarabangha Maharshi that he would help Rama and he flew to paradise. After Indra had flown, Sarabangha Maharshi came to the place where Sita and Laxmana were waiting along with Rama. They touched his feet and took his blessings and later he invited them into his ashram.

Rama asked Maharshi why Lord Indra had come there. Then Maharshi said that he had satisfied with my penance. So he blessed me with a boon. Indra also promised me that he would take me to heaven. But your arrival made my journey cancel. I will go after giving you hospitality, said Sarabangha Maharshi.

Later Rama enquired about the place. Then Maharshi told Suthiksha to live here. He would accompany you in everything. Now it is time for me, I left heaven. You cross the river Mandakini, there you will find Subhiksha, said Sarabangha Maharshi. Meanwhile Sarabangha Maharshi turned into light form and his physical body disappeared and the light flew to heaven.

After Sarabangha had gone to heaven, many hermits came to see Rama. They praised Rama and his dynasty. They said that they had heard the greatness of him. They told him that the king who treated his people as if they were his sons, would reach heaven. There he was also adored with fruits and stems. The king who torture his people with a lot of taxes, he would reach the hell and be punished.

They pleaded with Rama to save the Brahmans who were in Vanaprastha. Many of them were being killed brutally by rakshasas on the bank of Mandakini. They also said that they were unable to rescue those who were doing meditation. So we request you to save them, said the hermits.

Then Rama replied to them in this way, "You shouldn't request me. It is my duty to save them. The god gave me an opportunity to protect them. I knew, my exile also was useful to many. I will definitely kill all of the rakshasas" Rama promised them and told them to go to Suthiksha Maharshi.

They later started working for the ashram of Suthikshna. They crossed many beautiful places and rivers on the way to the ashram. The forest was filled with different species of trees and animals. They finally reached the ashram after a few hours of their journey on foot. Suthikshna, who was with long twisted hair, welcomed Rama, Laxmana and Sita. Rama introduced himself and he introduced his wife and brother. Rama also said that he had come to see him. Then Suthikshna felt very happy and embraced him.

Suthikshna said, "Rama! You are the man of righteousness. I am very happy to see you in my ashram. I was waiting for a long time. I pity your situation. Even Indra did not escape from the troubles like you" So make the exile useful and be happy with Sita and Laxmana.

Rama replied, "Maharshi! I was looking for a shelter in this forest. Sarabangha Maharshi told about you. With his advice of him, I came here"

Then Suthikshna said, "This ashram is so beautiful. Many priests and hermits are living here. You can find multi fruits and stems. This is a safe place to live in. Here violence of animals and humans are prohibited"

Rama replied that they were not going to live there permanently. They would spend only one night. Then Suthikshna said, "Okay" Rama, Laxmana and Sita spent happily in the ashram that night.

Next morning Rama, Laxmana and Sita met Suthikshna. They thanked him for giving accommodation to them in his ashram. They asked his permission to move further. When he asked to stay back for some time, Rama replied that they had to start before the sun shone. When the hermit gave them permission, they took his blessings.

Then they again started their journey. They were proceeding enjoying the beauty of nature. They were also enjoying the taste of fruits on the way. They found many lakes, tanks, ponds, brooks, waterfalls and rivers. They were enjoying birds' singing peacocks' dancing. Thus their journey was wonderful.

There they spent that night. Rama woke up in the early morning and did his morning routine. Later Rama, Laxmana and Sita decided to leave the place so they went to Suthikshna and told him that they were leaving the place. They said that they had come to him to take his permission. He gave them permission to go. Later they took his blessings and were about to start.

Then Suthikshna gave them some suggestions and directions. He advised them to protect themselves from cruel animals and weather. He also suggested that they enjoy the beauty of the forest. Then Rama said, "Okay" They later moved into the forest. While they were traveling, Sita told Rama how the society was filled with evils. Sita praised her husband's qualities. She felt her husband was the best man in the world. She knew the men in the society were full of lust.

Then Rama replied that it was his duty to protect the righteous. So many hermits are suffering from rakshasas in this forest. All are waiting for someone who will protect them. So it is our duty to protect them. When they reached a place, all the hermits were very happy to see Rama. They felt that they were going to be saved by him. Then Rama promised them that in any situation, he would not be going to leave his promise. To save them, he was ready to forgo Sita and Laxmana but he wouldn't live without saving them.

The hermits gave accommodation to Rama, Sita and Laxmana. They took a rest in the ashram that night. They woke up in the early morning. Rama and Laxmana went to the lake to take bath. When they were about to dip in the lake, the noise was heard. They looked around to know where the voice was coming from but they didn't see anyone. Then they went to the hermit named Dharmabrutha and asked him eagerly about the strange noise in the lake.

Then the hermit told him that it was the lake, Panchapsara. Here the hermit, Mandakarni had performed a great penance. Then lord Indra sent his five beautiful angels to him. They married the hermit, Mandakini. Then the hermit constructed a beautiful house beneath the lake. They sometimes dance there. The hermit said to Rama, "It might be the sound made by them" Then Rama was surprised to hear that. Later they took bath in the lake and performed their morning puja.

Thus, Rama, Sita and Laxmana were spending different ashrams and spending their time in the forest. Thus their ten years of forest life was completed. Later they came back to the ashram of Suthikshna, seeing different locations. They asked Suthikshna about Agasthya. Then Suthikshna told them about Agasthya. He suggested they visit the brother of Agasthya. "Later he will tell you about his brother," said Suthikshna.

Next they started to the ashram of Agasthya's brother. They reached the ashram and took his blessings. That evening they were accommodated in the ashram and in the night they were provided fruits and stems. That night they knew the way to the ashram of Agasthya. In the early morning after taking bath, they went to the ashram of Agasthya.

Laxmana went to Agasthya and told him in this way, "I am Laxmana. My brother Rama and his wife Sita are waiting outside. We are the sons of the king, Dasharatha. We came from Ayodhya. We are living in the forest as a part of exile for fourteen years" Then the hermit, Agasthya, felt very happy on Rama's arrival to his ashram. He had been waiting for his arrival for a long time. He told Laxmana to bring Rama and Sita in. It is not good for me to keep Rama waiting. Then Laxmana went back and brought Rama and Sita before Agasthya.

When Agasthya saw Rama and Sita, his heart felt thrilled. He felt as if he was looking at Lord Vishnu and Laxmi. Later Agasthya adored Rama along with his people in the ashram. He also provides them with fresh fruits and stems. After they received hospitality from Agasthya, Rama was told about the bow of Vishnu. Agasthya said, "With this bow, I killed so many rakshasas. It is the most powerful weapon. So now I want to present It to you so that you can use it wherever necessary. If it is used by you, no one can encounter you at the war"

Agasthya felt very happy for the sojourn of Rama, Laxmana and Sita. "Your departure is making me sad and I am worried mostly about Sita. She did not face any difficulties from her childhood. Now she is sauntering in the forest facing a lot of troubles. I suggest you take care of her otherwise she will be afraid of the cruel animals" said Agasthya.

Then Rama replied that he would definitely take care of her. He told that in fact it was his duty to look after her. Later Rama knew about the beautiful place called Panchavati. Agasthya suggested Rama to build a hut there and start living in it as it was the best place in the forest to live in. Agasthya was very happy with Rama's obedience. He said that he had not seen such a person in the world. Rama, Laxmana and Sita took blessings of Agasthya later they started towards Panchavati. They were surprised to look at the beautiful places and birds on their way to Panchavati.

Before they reached Panchavati, Rama and Laxmana had come across a big eagle named Jatayu. They thought that it might be a kind of giant. Then the eagle melodiously told them that it was their father's friend. Then Rama and Laxmana felt very happy to hear their father's name from the eagle. Rama had a suspicion about it and enquired about their dynasty. Then Jatayu started explaining their dynasty details.

It told the whole history of their dynasty which made Rama and Laxmana astonished. They later knew Jatayu was their friend and not an enemy. Jatayu promised them that it was its duty to take care of Sita. Then Rama and Laxmana had a complete belief in it.

Rama showed Panchavati to Laxmana and Sita. He suggested Laxmana to search for a better place to build Parnasala. Then Laxmana watched the surroundings and decided to build Parnasala where the multicolored flowers are grown. Just beside the place there is the river Godavari. Even Agasthya told them about the place. Different species of birds and animals were also found there.

So Laxmana built a beautiful Parnasala within a few hours. Rama and Sita felt very happy to see the beautiful hut. They appreciated his hard work and talent. After slaughtering an animal, they entered the hut with utmost happiness. They later lived in it happily for a few days.

One day Rama went to take bath in the river Godavari along with his wife. Laxmana also accompanied them. Laxmana told Rama, "Bharatha is doing a great penance. He forfeited all the luxuries and lived like a lay man for his mother's misdeeds. He who lived his life luxuriously, now leading a very normal life like us" Rama felt very low for Bharatha's decision at the same time he felt very proud for having him as his brother. After they had taken a bath, they went back to their hut.

After they had taken a bath in the river, they went back to their hut. That day they spent happily in Panchavati with the hermits. Later Rama spent some time with Sita savouring the beauty of the moon light at night. While they were in the conversation, a rakshasi came to the place. She is Shurpanka, the sister of Ravan. She saw the handsome Rama and craved for him with the feeling of lust. She also questioned Rama how he had come to their place with his wife.

Rama told everything and explained how he had come to the place. He also questioned her who she was. She also told everything about her. After that she told him that she had liked him very much and pleaded with him to marry her. She warned Rama if he rejects her proposal, she would kill and eat his brother, Laxmana. She also told him to come along with her to her place and there they would enjoy looking at the beauty of nature.

Then Rama replied to lustful Shurpanka, "I am married and I love my wife. I don't agree with your proposal and make her sad by doing sinful things. My brother is unmarried and he is very handsome. He is a suitable match to you. You can have him as your husband" On hearing the words of Rama, Shurpanka was convinced. She went to Laxmana and asked him to marry her.

Laxmana laughed at once on hearing her words. He said, "I am not suitable for you. Marry my brother, he is only the best husband for you. You can be a second wife to him though he is married. He definitely leaves his old wife and marries you as you are looking fantastic. He loves you very much" Then Shurpanka went to Rama again and asked him to marry her. She said that she would kill and eat Sita, later she would marry him. She also said that she would look after Rama very well in the forest.

Shurpanka next saw Sita with much anger and went to kill her. Then Laxmana came to Sita's rescue. He held a sharp sword and cut off both her ears and nose. Shurpanka was frightened and ran away to her place crying. She went to Khara, the leader of Rakshasas and complained to him about what had happened. Then Khara got angry with Rama and Laxmana. He immediately went to Panchavati to kill them for Laxmana's misdeed.

Before Khara started to Panchavati, he knew that his sister was hurt by Laxmana. His heart felt very sad after looking at her pathetic condition. He promised Shurpanka that he would kill them and take revenge on them for hurting her. He described himself as a great being in the area and stated that no one would defeat him. Khara went with his fellow rakshasas who were very strong. They went to Panchavati to attack Rama and Laxmana.

When they went, Rama, Sita and Laxmana were resting in Parnasala. They suddenly came into the hut. Then Rama told Laxmana to take care of Sita meanwhile he would fight with them and send them away. Rama took his golden powerful bow and shot at them with powerful arrows. Khara challenged Rama that he will be defeated. Khara and his fellow rakshasas threw Shulas at them. Rama defended the shulas with his powerful arrows. And Rama immediately sent his numerous arrows at them. With them all the rakshasas fell onto the earth.

One of the rakshasas went to Khara and told him about the faintness of their fellows. Then Khara and the leader of his army, Dushanbe went toward Rama and Laxmana to directly fight with him. Along with them about fourteen thousands of rakshasas went to engage in the war. They were roaring like thunder.

While they were moving the sounds of foxes trembled Khara. He suspected what it might be. He felt that something inauspicious things are going to be happened. But he did not go back. He darley resumed what they had felt earlier. On the other hand, Rama stood darley to fight with them. All the hermits and priests blessed him that he would win the war and slaughter them. Later Rama and Laxmana were surrounded by the rakshasas army as if it was the sun's eclipse.

Later, the rakshasas threw all their Shulas at Rama and Laxmana. But without fear, Rama and Laxmana defended them with their powerful arrows. And in excess they used their arrows which made rakshasas terrified. They removed the armours of rakshasas. Thus Rama and Laxmana killed a large number of rakshasas in the war. They were frightened at the skill of Rama and fled back to Khara to save them from him. Rama's arrow of Gandharva terrified them.

Then Khara ordered his soldiers to counter Rama as he was creating the horror. He ordered his army to kill him first so that they will be safe. Then their army went towards Rama. Khara's army threw thousands of arrows at Rama. Then Rama turned his bow in 360 degrees and shot powerful astras at them. With them all the rakshasas' armour fell onto the ground. Later the different astras killed their elephants and horses. The chariots and soldiers were sunk into the ground. The soldiers who were alive went to Khara to rescue them from Rama, the warrior.

The soldiers, who attacked on Rama, went to the Yama Loka. Then Dushana consoled them and prepared the other soldiers to fight with the two brothers. With the motivation of Dushana, the remaining soldiers went towards Rama to kill him. Then there was a terrible fight between Rama and rakshasas. All the rakshasas surrounded Rama. Doing nothing, it was inadundate for him to use Gandharva astra. When it was used the earth made a terrible sound.

Later Dushana himself went towards Rama. Rama immediately killed his horses and cut off Dushana's hands which made him fall onto the ground. Within a few minutes Dushana and his army succumbed to injuries made by Rama. Then Khara was very much angry with Rama. He took twelve giants along with him to fight with Rama. And Rama could easily kill them with his powerful weapons. Rama alone killed about fourteen thousands of soldiers in the war.

After Trisharasa had died, even Khara was terrified with the power of Rama. But he didn't hesitate to encounter him. Both fought ferociously in the war. Khara tried to break the bow of Rama with his sword. Khara even hurt Rama with his powerful weapons. Rama's armour fell onto the ground. Then Rama took the bow of Vaishnava and used it against Khara. He shot his first arrow which made Khara's flag onto the ground. Later Rama destroyed their chariots, horses and elephants. That made Khara stand on the ground. Then all the gods appeared from heaven and blessed Rama for his heroic action in the war.

Khara boasted himself that he was a great warrior and ridiculed Rama for killing just normal rakshasas. Khara challenged Rama if he had dared enough to kill him. Then Khara threw his weapon, Gadha, upon Rama. Rama simply defended that and it immediately smashed. Rama later threw many arrows which pricked in the body of Khara. The blood started pouring out like a stream. Later Rama burnt Khara's dead body with his arrow of fire. Thus Khara's episode was finished.

The gods from heaven showered flowers on Rama for killing more than fourteen thousands of rakshasas. Lord Indra came to the ashram where Rama was living in and appreciated Rama. Sita and Laxmana felt very proud of Rama.

One of the rakshasas who was not dead in the war, went to Lanka and told Ravana, "Oh! honourable king, our people were brutally killed in the war. Even our Khara was also killed" Then the ten headed Ravana was furious and raged. He angrily asked who he was. Ravana said, "How dare he? The ones who had done harm to me, wouldn't live anymore. Even lord Indra and Yama had to face the music. I have the capacity of burning the sun" The rakshas told Ravana that it was Rama who killed their fellow rakshasas in the war.

Then Ravana felt that the gods might have sent Rama to kill our people. The raakshas told Ravana about Rama's skills at the war. He stated that our people would not stand before Rama. He also told Ravana about his brother, Laxmana. He was explaining to Ravana how both the brothers engaged in war and killed their people. Then Ravana was furious and promised that he would kill both the brothers for killing his people.

Then the rakshas explained the greatness of Rama. He stated that no one would face him. That made Ravana angry. Then the rakshas gave an idea of killing Rama. He talked about his wife Sita, who is very beautiful. If she is abducted, Rama will definitely die himself as he wouldn't live without her. Then Ravana was very happy with the idea of the rakshas.

Immediately Ravana started on his chariot to abduct Sita. On the way, he met Maricha. Maricha felicitated Ravana for coming to his place after a long time. Then they discussed Rama and Ravana told him the purpose of visiting the land. Ravana asked for the help to abduct Sita from the clutches of Rama. Then Maricha enquired how Ravana had got the idea of abducting Sita. Maricha objected to his idea of abducting and suggested he look after his wives instead of doing this sinful thing.

After Maricha had suggested to Ravana not to abduct Sita, Ravana went back to Lanka. But Shurpanka went to Lanka and she provoked her brother to abduct Sita. Shurpanka was very furious about the deaths of their fellows and about her humiliation made by the two brothers. She explained Ravana about his greatness. She questioned him why he wouldn't kill and abduct Sita. She reminded his conquests over the gods. But Ravana did not move with her words.

Then Shurpanka got angry with her brother, Ravana. She started scolding him for his attitude towards his people. She questioned why he remained silent while his people were dying in huge numbers. She stated that he was an inefficient king to his people. A king should stand for the people. He shouldn't hesitate to take revenge on his enemies. She explained the greatness of Rama and how he is fulfilling the duties allotted by the gods. Why her brother was not like Rama and he did not have the qualities as Rama had. She was trying to provoke her brother and wanted to commit sin that is abducting Sita from the clutches of Rama. And she wanted to take revenge on the two brothers for humiliating her.

Ravana asked Shurpanka, "Who is Rama? How much strength does he has? What is his weapon?"

Shurpanka said, "Rama is the son of the king, Dasharatha. He is now in exile for fourteen years due to fulfilling his father's promise. He is a very good warrior. He alone killed fourteen thousands of people. Now he became the hero for the hermits in the forest. He has a beautiful wife and her name is Sita. She is suitable for you. Marry her so that your reputation will grow. Rama's brother, Laxmana, took off my clothes with force. The two brothers insulted me. So take revenge on them for ridiculed and teased your sister"

Ravana then was convinced with his sister's words and decided to take revenge on Rama for teasing his sister and killing his soldiers in huge numbers. Later he went to the place where Maricha lives. Maricha again welcomed him and gave good accommodation. Later he enquired his purpose of coming to him. Ravana completely explained what had happened to his army and his sister, Shurpanka. Later, Ravana asked for Maricha's help for abducting Sita. Maricha asked how he could help him. Then Ravana told him to be in disguise as a golden deer and saunter before Sita so that she would feel that you are the real deer. Then she craves for the deer and her husband will follow the deer. At that moment, I will disguise myself as a beggar and go for alms to their hut. When Sita comes out, I will abduct her. Ravana's plan shocked Maricha. Maricha felt that it would not be good to be a part of the crime.

Maricha requested Ravana not to abduct Sita. He opined that Rama is a very good person. If we do that, he will also kill us. Rama is the form of righteousness. If we withdraw our plan, we will be saved. If you want to take revenge, fight with Rama but not the abduction of Sita.

Ravana objected to the option of Maricha. He ordered just to follow what he had said. He ordered Maricha to disguise as the golden deer and stimulate Sita so that Rama will follow you. If you succeed in that, I will give you half of my kingdom. Without war, I will kill Rama, said Ravana.

Doing nothing, Maricha disguised himself as the golden deer. Ravana had shown the hut of Rama. He asked him to go and stand there. As Ravana said, Maricha started roaming in front of Parnasala. At the time, Sita was plucking flowers for her puja. Then Maricha went towards Sita and stood there until Sita saw him. After some time, Sita's eyes had fallen on the golden deer. She was very much surprised to look at the deer.

Laxmana observed the scene and called her into the hut. Then Sita said, "See! "The beautiful golden deer" I want that " Then Laxmana said that it was a Black magic made by the rakshasas. He also told her that it was not a real deer. But Sita didn't listen to him. Anyhow, "I need that", Sita said. Since Sita wanted it, Rama called Jatayu and told him to look after Sita until he returns. "I will go and kill it with my arrow", said Rama. Rama also orders Laxmana to take care of Sita and not go anywhere leaving her alone in the hut.

Laxmana said, "Ok"

Then Rama took his bow and arrows and went in the direction of the deer. The deer started its magic. It sometimes is appearing to him, sometimes not. When it appeared to him, he with utmost concentration shot at the deer. With the shot, the deer fell onto the ground as the powerful arrows were pierced into its body. Then the deer cried Sita! Laxmana! It was crying like Rama. When it was dead, it was looking like a giant. Then Rama understood that it was somebody's plot against them. Rama recollected Laxmana's word and he felt very sorry for not listening to him. Rama thought that Sita and Laxmana feel that it was his sound. Then he rushed to the hut with its meat.

Sita heard the voice of her husband and she thought something had happened to her husband. She immediately ordered Laxmana to check if it was Rama. "If he is in danger, go and save him", said Sita. But Laxmana said that his brother had ordered him not to leave his wife in any situation. So he said that he wouldn't go anywhere and he opined that was the magic voice made like his brother. Sita was very furious with Laxmana. She questioned if he was interested to see his brother's mishap. When Sita cried for Rama, Laxmana tried to move into the forest to save his brother.

But Laxmana had confidence that Rama was not in danger. But he worried about Sita for listening to his words. Sita was not listening to him. So, Laxmana decided to go but on one condition. He said that he would draw up a line, even in unavoidable circumstances, she would not cross it. Sita agreed and went into the forest in search of Rama.

After Laxmana had gone, Ravana appeared at the place. He laughed, everything was going as he planned. He was ready to use the situation to his advantage. Then Ravana was disguised as a priest and called Sita for alms. When she came out he was appreciating her beauty but Sita did not move. Ravana continued that Sita was attracted to him and exclaimed that he had not seen such beauty in his life. He told that she shouldn't be in the forest but should be with him in the palace. Since Sita thought he was a priest, she treated him as her guest. She knew, "The guest is god" Then Ravana tried to abduct her. But Sita was looking into the forest if Laxmana was coming along with her husband.

Sita was frightened by Ravana's teasing words. He was continuously bullying her. Then Sita asked what his gothram was and if he was really a brahmin. She opined, a real brahmin never teases a woman. Then Ravana introduced himself to be a great king of Lanka. Ravana said that he started loving her at the very first sight. He said, "After seeing you, I started hating my wives and my love for them disappeared. Your beauty is equal to the beauty of five thousand women. So you can come with me and be my wife. You will be treated as my dear wife in the palace.

Then Sita was angry with Ravana. She told him that she was the wife of the great Rama. My husband is equal to Lord Indra. My husband is a lion and you are a fox. There is a lot of difference between my husband and you. If you crave for me, it will be like putting your hand in the snake's mouth and jumping into the ocean tying a big rock to the waist. Then Ravana laughed loudly and started explaining the greatness of him. He said that Kubera was his brother. Sita warned him it was okay touching the wife of Lord Indra but if he touched the wife of Rama, he would be turned into ashes.

Ravana asked Sita to come out of threshold and give him alms. Sita rejected his proposal. He said that when a priest comes to your house, will you send him without offering alms? He said that it would be a sin. Then Sita tried to come out of the line, drawn by Laxmana. But she suddenly recollected Laxmana's words. She refused to come out. When Ravana tried to go inside, the sudden fire from the line drawn by Laxmana came out. Ravana was afraid to look at the fire.

Then Ravana was very angry with Sita's behaviour. He forced her to come out and to perform alms. Then Sita thought that it would not be nice to send him without giving alms. As soon as Sita crossed the line, Ravana changed into his original form. Sita was frightened to see his giant form and ten big heads. Then he came forward and touched the thigh of Sita. He called for his chariot and it appeared before them. Immediately he dragged Sita into it. Then Sita started shouting to save her. Meanwhile the chariot flew into the air. Sita and Rama! Laxmana! Ravana is abducting me, "Save me" cried Sita. Ravana was laughing as his plan was successful and he told Sita that she must face the music as her husband's had done a great damage to them.

Sita did not notice anyone on their way. So she told the river Godavari to tell her husband about the abduction. Jatayu heard the cries of Sita and he flew up to the chariot. Sita saw Jatayu and felt very happy. She thought she would be saved by Jatayu.

Jatayu told Ravana that it would be a sin to abduct Sita who is the wife of Rama. He suggested Ravana to leave Sita immediately and act according to the righteousness. He said that Sita was in the form godess Laxmi. But Ravana made a deaf ear. Jatayu's words did not reach into his ears. Ravana laughed at Jatayu and said to him that he was not going to leave her. Then Jatayu told him if he was not ready to leave her, he would be going to face consequences. Ravana told with pride that no one would conquer him and he declared himself to be greater than trinity.

Jatayu challenged Ravana to win over him and take Sita. He said, "Though I am very old and you are young, I am ready to fight with you to save Sita. While I am alive and I would not let you take Sita" Then Ravana agreed to fight with Jatayu. Though Jatayu was a small creature before Ravana, he fought bravely with him. Jatayu defended all the arrows of Ravana and spoiled his chariot and pierced with his beak all over his body. Jatayu also killed the donkeys which were driving the chariot.

Later Ravana and Sita had fallen onto the ground. Ravana got furious on Jatayu and he took his sharp sword from his dagger and cut off Jatayu's wings at once. With that Jatayu had fallen onto the ground and died later. Sita then started crying loudly looking at the dead body of Jatayu. She blamed herself because Jatayu had died because of her. Sita started calling Rama! Rama! Then Ravana held her hair tightly and started his journey to Lanka. With that awful thing, the light had disappeared and the hermits felt very sad for this untoward happening. They also felt Ravana's death was about to happen. Meanwhile Ravana flew into the sky, holding Sita.

Sita blamed Ravana while he was taking her away from her husband. She treated him as a human animal. She pointed her finger at him and said in a solemn voice; "If my husband was present there, you would become a corpse" She also reminded Ravana that her husband alone killed Ravana's fourteen thousand soldiers for attacking her husband. She warned him lastly to leave her at that moment otherwise he must face the consequence but Ravana did not care her words.

Sita couldn't do anything. She was trying to let loose herself from the clutches of Ravana but he held her firmly. So she gave up. When they were flying, Sita saw five monkey men in the forest. So she dropped her jewels before the monkey men without being noticed by Ravana. The money men saw Ravana abducting Sita. They felt very sad while Ravana crossed the sea and entered Lanka. He kept her in a private palace and ordered the rakshasas to look after her.

Ravana also told rakshasas to give whatever Sita asks. Then he thought of killing Rama so that his enmity would be fulfilled. For that he sent eight rakshasas to kill Rama. After killing Rama, Ravana thought of marrying Sita. Later Ravana asked to fulfil his lust but Sita sat among the rakshasas and started crying. Then he boasted about himself and his wealth. He forcefully showed his palace. Though he boasted himself and offered the queenship of Lanka, Sita simply rejected his proposal.

Then Sita started telling the greatness of her husband. She simply stated that Ravana was lesser than Rama in every aspect and more Rama had a good character. And he never looked at the others' wives with the desire of lust. She also talked about the greatness of Laxmana. "If they know about my abduction, they can kill you", said Sita. She also warned him that he was going to die soon. Ravana laughed at her mock warnings. He told Sita that he was giving her a chance to think about his proposal for a year. "After that I will not see you talking like this' ', said Ravana. He also ordered the female raakshasas to torture her until she accepts with his proposal.

So the rakshasas took her to Ashoka garden. There Sita was imprisoned. They were daily torturing Sita. Sita bore everything but she did not surrender to them. Every day she was crying for Rama.

Lord Indra came to know about the abduction of Sita by Ravana. He felt very sad about that. Indra immediately went to Lord Brahma and told about the incident. He told Brahma Sita had been abducted for the welfare of the hermits and to kill the rakshasas but Sita was crying continuously without having food and water. She was worrying about her husband and waiting for him to take her back. "If she continues that, she will die", said Indra.

Then Lord Brahma responded positively and promised that he would take care of Sita. Brahma told Indra that Rama would go to Lanka and kill Ravana. Then Indra felt very happy. But he questioned how Sita would live without eating. Brahma then gave him ambrosia and told him to give it to Sita.

Indra went to Lanka in disguise and offered ambrosia to Sita. Sita at first did not recognize him but after Indra had shown his original form, she took and had ambrosia. Indra told her that Rama and Laxmana would definitely come and take you back after killing Ravana.

Sita was very happy to know the details of Rama and

Laxmana. She requested Indra to be helpful to her husband and his brother. Indra promised her that he would be with him at every situation. Sita felt very happy with Indra's promise. Later Sita got confidence and stopped crying. Indra took leave from Sita and went to Indraloka. The rakshasas surprised to see the sudden change in Sita.

Rama on the other hand went into the deep forest to kill the golden deer. There he noticed that it was not a deer but it was Maricha who deliberately came in disguise. He killed Maricha with his arrows and started coming back to his Parnasala. On the way, he heard the cries of foxes. He felt that something had happened to Sita. He also heard Maricha crying like him while dying. While Rama was returning, he came across his brother who was coming hurriedly for Rama. Rama asked Laxmana why he had left Sita alone in the hut. "I feel this is an inauspicious time and the rakshasas may cause trouble to Sita ", said Rama.

Rama thus worried about Sita if Sita had been in trouble. Later Rama and Laxmana rushed to Parnasala and they were astonished to find the absence of Sita in the hut. Rama blamed Laxmana for leaving his wife alone though he instructed not to leave her alone. Rama broke into tears and felt very sad. He couldn't bear the situation. His loving wife's absence in the hut made him bore the brunt. He was crying continuously.

Rama asked Laxmana repeatedly why he had left Sita alone in Parnasala. Then Laxmana told his brother that Sita herself had pleaded with him to go into the forest to save her husband. "Even I heard the voice of you. It said that you are in danger. Sita continuously provoked me to come to save you in the forest. I told her that no one would harm or kill you but with a lot of love on you, she pleaded with me to save you. So it has become an inevitable situation for me. When I refused to go, she blamed me that I was looking for death you. Since she suspected me, I came into the forest" Laxmana told Rama.

Then Rama questioned Laxmana how he would simply care for the words of a lady without looking for her protection. Then where his words had gone to take care of her before entering the forest to kill the deer?

Finally they let the topic go. Rama told "Whatever had happened had happened; now there was no use of talking. Let's look for Sita. Where had she gone? What happened to her? Did anyone do harm to her? Let's go and ask anyone who is on the way or else we can ask the trees and the rivers about her", Rama said to Laxmana.

They searched for Sita but did not find the evidence of Sita. They looked in all the directions. They asked the trees and the river Godavari but no use. Nobody replied to them. Rama cried as there was no reply from anyone. He felt what he would tell her father when he asked about his daughter. Laxaman went in the direction of the South as the animals were looking at the south. Rama also followed Laxmana in that direction. After they had travelled for several miles, they saw the flowers on the ground. Rama recognized the flowers which were usually worn by his wife, Sita. So Rama asked the hills and brooks whether they had seen his wife.

Then the hills told him that two people fought each other for a lady. "We don't whether she was Sita", they said. They had shown the evidences of the fight. Rama saw the remnants of bow and other weapons. He also saw the dead bodies of donkeys. Rama cried that the rakshasas took revenge on him by abducting Sita. Rama pleaded the gods to tell the information about his wife otherwise he would smash the whole world. "If they give back his wife, he can kill all the rakshasas", said Rama. Rama raged and his eyes turned into red. He is looking as lord Rudra.

Then Laxmana tried to appease him. He prostrated not to get furious. He told that Rama was conquered over all his senses. It would not be fine to show his anger which will cause damage to the society. He, who has to protect the world, will not cause damage. So Laxmana appeased with his words. "It is not that we should spoil the world, it is the time to search for Sita", said Laxmana. He requested Rama to behave well.

Rama was appeased with soothing words of Laxmana. He felt that it was good to be patient. He decided to search for Sita but he doesn't know where and how to search. He asked his brother, "How can we find Sita?" With that Laxmana thought for a while and came up with an idea that they would go in the same direction as they found some evidence. After they had travelled for some more miles, they found Jatayu, lying on the ground. Laxmana thought that Jatayu might have killed Sita and he immediately was about to shoot it. Just then, he found Jatayu shedding blood.

On seeing Rama, Jatayu told that Ravana had abducted Sita. He told that he had tried his level best to let loose Sita but Ravana cut off his wings. Then Laxmana felt very sad for thinking badly about Jatayu and he started crying. Rama went to Jatayu and hugged him. Rama felt miserable for the troubles he had continuously. Rama and Laxmana felt unhappy for his father's friend's pathetic condition.

Seeing Jatayu, Rama spoke with Laxmana in this way, "This Jayatu has fought for me. Though his strength is less, he fought with the strong Ravana. I really pity him" Rama asked Jatayu about Sita and what had happened to her. How did Ravana steal her? What harm did I do to him? He asked several questions about Sita and Ravana. Then Jatayu opened his mouth and told Rama everything, how Ravana abducted and how he cut off his wings. Jatayu also told Rama not to worry about Sita. She will come back after Ravana is killed by you. He told Rama that Ravana was the brother of Kubota. While Jatayu was speaking, he vomited blood and died later.

Rama cried looking at the corpse of Jatayu. He has been living in the forest for a long time. And he died today because of Rama. Jatayu from then was worshipped as he aided Sita. Rama ordered Laxmana to bring the dried wood for the pyre. They placed Jatayu on the pyre and did his cremation according to the rituals. Later Rama and Laxmana prayed for his soul to rest in peace in heaven. Later they took bath in the Godavari and started travelling further in search of Sita.

They went deeper into the forest. They crossed many ashrams and encountered many cruel animals. They found a hill in the middle of the forest and it had a cave. They entered the cave and there they saw a giant. The giant terrified them with its wicked body. It ridiculed Laxmana which made him raged. Laxmana went to him and cut off his ears and nose with his sharp sword.

Laxmana suggested Rama to be careful as his left arm was shaking. Meanwhile the terrible sound terrified them. His hands are very long and had an eye in the stomach. To their surprise, he had no head. He was simply sitting in the giant chair and dragging animals and keeping them in his stomach. Laxmana was afraid to look at him. Then Rama soothed him not to be afraid of the giant. The giant introduced himself. He said that he was Kabandha. He said not to be afraid of him. He told Rama if he is buried by Rama, they would get the power of sixth sense.

Rama and Laxmana buried and cremated him and Kabandha immediately changed into Gandharva. Kabandha once was Gandharva because of the curse, he turned into a giant. That day his curse was redeemed by Rama. As Rama helped him, Gandharva told to make friendship with Sugreeva. "Sugreeva will be helpful to you in searching Sita", said Gandharva.

Kabandha who is now Gandharva told Rama that there was a river called Pampa. You go there and leave your misery at the bank of the river. One more thing is Sabari, an old lady has been waiting for you for a long time. After seeing you, she will join the heaven choir. From there, you can go to the hill, Rishyamukha. The hill contained a cave which was covered with rocks. In the cave, Sugreeva, Vanara king is residing. Go and meet him. Make friendship with him as he is very nice and humble. He will be helpful to you in searching for Sita. Later Gandharva flew to heaven.

CHAPTER FOUR

Kishkindakanda

As Gandharva said, Rama and Laxmana started their journey towards the river Pampa. They reached Sabari ashram and took blessings of her. Sabari was on cloud nine, looking at Rama. She gave them nice accommodation and hospitality. Sabari asked the welfare of Rama and shot at him plenty of questions. Sabari was very happy to see him in her ashram.

Sabari later adored Rama with much devotion. She spent some time with Rama and Laxmana. Later she slept in the lap of Rama and changed into the light form. That light went to heaven. After Sabari had defected, Rama told Laxmana, "We are very grateful to be here and experienced wonderful memories with Sabari" They later started their journey towards Rishyamukha Hill.

Rama and Laxmana reached the river Pampa and were surprised to look at the beauty of the surroundings but his sadness was haunting him. He told Laxmana that he had been suffering due to Kaikeyi. She sent him and his wife to the forest. "Now she is abducted which made me very unhappy. But the place subsided my sadness a little. The hills, flowers and birds are looking so fantastic", said Rama.

Then the king of Vanara, Sugreeva, was sauntering in the area. He saw Rama and Laxmana and was surprised. He didn't know who they were. He felt that they were aliens. He thought that they would do harm to them. He immediately went back to his place and there he told his ministers that the enemies sent by Vali were roaming in their area. He also told them that they came in disguise to smash their kingdom. Then the ministers decided to go to Rama and Laxmana to know who they were.

After some time, the ministers went to the place where Rama and Laxmana were staying. They were afraid of Rama and Laxmana as they might be the men of Vali. Then one of Sugreeva's ministers, Hanuman, told them that they were not the men of Vali. So don't be afraid of Vali, he won't do anything, said Hanuman. The people of Vali do not contain long arms and legs. They look like very clever men. Then Sugreeva ordered Hanuman to go to them and enquire who they were. Then Hanuman decided to converse with Rama and Laxmana.

Before Hanuman went to meet Rama and Laxmana, he had changed into the form of a saint. Hanuman went to them and at first he introduced himself. Later he asked them who they were. Hanuman also asked them where they had come from. "The animals are roaming here. Are you not afraid of them?" asked Hanuman.

Though Hanuman was asking them questions repeatedly, Rama and Laxmana did not utter a word and they looked Hanuman in surprise. Then Hanuman told about Sugreeva that his brother, Vali had done harm to him. Now Sugreeva was roaming in the forest with the grief. "Sugreeva sent me here to know about you. I am Hanuman, his minister.

My father is the god of wind. Since Sugreeva requested me, I came in the form of the saint. I came from the hill of Rishyamukha" said Hanuman.

Then Rama felt very happy and he introduced himself and his brother to Hanuman. Then Hanuman engaged in conversation with them which made Rama very happy. Rama was also surprised with the oratory, fluency and accuracy of the language of Hanuman. Hanuman knew all the Vedas which made Rama and Laxmana astonished. Rama stated that Sugreeva was very fortunate to have Hanuman as his minister. Such ministers can perform any difficult activity with much ease.

Then Laxmana spoke with Hanuman in this way, "Hanuman, the scholar! We are also looking for Sugreeva. We will be helpful to him" Hanuman was elated with the words of Laxmana. Then he decided to unite Rama and Sugreeva.

Later Hanuman took Rama and Sita to Sugreeva. He felt that Sugreeva would get back his kingdom definitely. While they were traveling Hanuman asked them how they had come to the dense forest. Then Rama told Laxmana to explain their story to Hanuman.

Then Laxmana spoke with Hanuman in this way, "Dasharatha, the king of Ayodhya was our father. He was ruling the country fairly. All the people were very happy with his rule. Rama is the elder son and I am Rama's younger brother. Rama is the most truthful and righteous in the world. He looks after all the living beings on the earth. He didn't even care about the king for the sake of our father's promise. Now we are in exile for fourteen years.

During our exile my brother's wife, Sita was abducted by Ravana. Kabandha told us that Sugreeva would help us in finding Sita. So we came here to meet Sugreeva"

Then Hanuman felt sad by knowing their pathetic story. He thought, "Great people came to take the help of my king, Sugreeva. Everyone has to take the help of Rama but now he is in need. How fate decided like this? Sugreeva is very lucky for being helpful to Rama" Hanuman shed tears for Rama's situation.

"The great people like you came for Sugreeva. He will definitely help you. He is also in need now. His brother, Vali abducted his wife. Now two brothers became enemies. You should help him in getting back his wife. We all search for Sita" said Hanuman.

Laxmana was very happy with Hanuman's kind heart. He told Rama that Hanuman became a part of us in searching for Sita. Hanuman doesn't tell lies and it seems he is an honest man. Later Hanuman came into his original form that is Vanara and took them to Sugreeva.

They reached their cave where Sugreeva was sitting on his throne. Hanuman told everything about Rama and Laxmana. He also explained how Rama had been abducted. "Now they came for your help in rescuing Sita. They came to know that Ravana had abducted her. These two brothers are equal to gods so we should adore and pray to them", said Hanuman.

Then Sugreeva came down from the platform and held Rama's hand and embraced him as a friendly gesture. Then all the vanaras welcomed Rama and Laxmana into their cave on the flowers' path which was arranged by Hanuman. Rama accepted their hospitality and made friendship with Sugreeva. They made Rama sit on the branch of the grape fruit tree after it was cut off and another branch for Laxmana.

Sugreeva then started narrating his story to Rama. He said that he had been sauntering in the forest with the threat of my elder brother. "Vali had abducted my wife, unable to encounter him, I had hidden myself in this cave. So please help in getting back my wife" Sugreeva said.

Then Rama smiled at him and promised that he would kill Vali for abducting your wife. With my powerful weapons, I will kill him so do not worry. Then Sugreeva felt very happy for the soothing words of Rama. Hanuman felt very happy for Rama and Sugreeva. As he wanted, both became friends.

Sugreeva was elated to hear the words of Rama. He saluted Rama with reverence. Later Sugreeva promised that he had not known anything about Ravana. "Even I did not know where he lived, what religion he belonged to. He also requested Rama to subside his grief for Sita. He had a hope that he would definitely kill Ravana and get back Sita. So be with dareness. Even though I am in the same situation but didn't get disheartened. I will be helpful to you. Let's take revenge on our enemies" said Sugreeva.

Thus Sugreeva consoled Rama and Rama could get back to normalcy. Rama felt that Sugreeva could play the role of a friend. He knew a friend's role is very important in everyone's life. So Rama felt very lucky to have Sugreeva as his friend. Rama told that he would be helpful to him and in the same way Sugreeva would be helpful to him. Rama assured him that he will not speak lies and he had not spoken before and ever. Everyone knows that he is the man of truth and righteousness.

Later Sugreeva spoke with Rama in this way, "Hanuman has told me that you are in exile for fourteen years and you have also worried about your wife. I will definitely help you in retrieving her. She might be anywhere in the world or above the world or beneath the world. It is my duty to take her back. I had a suspicion that I saw a lady a few days back, she might be Sita. That lady was crying Rama and Laxmana repeatedly. She dropped her jewels while somebody was taking her in the sky. I collected those jewels and kept them safely"

Then Rama asked to show him the jewels with much eagerness. Sugreeva went into his cave immediately and got them back and showed them to Rama. Rama identified Utharabaranam and he exclaimed that it belonged to his wife. He cried at once on seeing the jewel. And Laxmana identified her anklets and rings. "Oh! It must be Ravana who took Sita", said Laxmana.

Rama asked Sugreeva to give the information about Ravana. He also asked in which direction they went. Where that person lived but Sugreeva told that he had known nothing about Ravana. Sugreeva felt very sad for not giving information which Rama asked.

Later Sugreeva cut off another branch which was full of beautiful flowers. They sat on the branch and Hanuman sat on the other branch. Then Sugreeva wanted to share something with Rama. Rama knew that Sugreeva wanted to speak with him. He asked Sugreeva to speak freely with him.

Sugreeva said, "My brother is threatening me. I have a life threat from him. So I have hidden myself in the cave. He has abducted my wife. So please save me from him and see that my wife will be free from him. You are my friend and my enemy is your enemy" Rama then was convinced with the explanation of Sugreeva and he promised him that he would kill his brother with his arrows.

Sugreeva felt very happy with the reply of Rama and he continued in this way, "My brother kicked out me from the kingdom and stole my wife. He has been waiting for the chance to kill me. These vanaras are protecting me in the forest. If my brother dies, I will be very happy. We are also happy "

Rama told him that feel that his enemy had died. Once I gave an assurance, no one would prevent that. I have the ability to kill Vali. Then Sugreeva got the courage and he felt that his grandeur life will be revived. And Sugreeva was ready to fight with his brother, Vali.

Sugreeva observed Rama and told him, "Rama! You should kill my brother with your bow and arrows. I will be very happy" Rama then embraced Sugreeva and suggested to him to make a move to Kishkinda later he would follow them. And there you invite Vali to the war. Meanwhile we come there and hide behind the trees, said Rama.

As said by Rama, Sugreeva went to Kishkinda and called Vali to the war. Vali with anger participated in the war. The two brothers fought ferociously. Rama on the other hand, wore his bow and observed their fight. While they were fighting, Rama couldn't identify Vali as they both looked alike. So he didn't shoot the arrow.

After some time, Sugreeva was unable to bear Vali's strength, ran away into his house. Vali beat him black and blue. Vali left his brother without killing him. After that Rama and Laxmana went to Sugreeva. Sugreeva felt ashamed of himself. And he asked Rama why he had not killed his brother, Vali.

Rama said to him not to get angry. He said that he couldn't identify who is who as both were looking alike. Then Rama told him to again fight with Vali but this time he had to wear the garland so that he could identify him. Sugreeva agreed with the proposal of Rama. He wore the garland and went to Vali again. Vali again came out of his palace and started fighting with Sugreeva.

For a few hours, the terrible fight had occurred between Vali and Sugreeva. Again Vali was becoming very strong and beating Sugreeva like anything. Then Rama shot an arrow at Vali which straight away pierced in the heart of Vali. With that Vali fell onto the ground at once and later went into an unconscious state. Then Rama went to Vali and he noticed that Vali was at the edge of death. Vali opened eyes and told Rama, "Do you feel that it is your greatness to kill from behind? You are a man with good qualities. Is it good to backstab? Vali asked adamantly why Rama had done like that?"

Srirama started giving explanations to Vali for killing him from the backside. "You are blaming me in anger. I have killed you for not standing on righteousness. You have abducted your brother's wife who is equal to your sister.

That was a sin. So you have been punished in this way. Being a Kshathriya, I can't bear your sin. Sugreeva is like my brother Laxmana. We kill wild animals which are cruel and you have also behaved like an animal so I killed you"

Vali reciprocated in this way, "I ask my apologies for behaving so. I have a son named Angadha. Please protect him. I fought with my Sugreeva and it is going to end with my death" Rama then consoled him not to worry about the mistake he committed. This act will sweep all of your sins. Now you will join the heaven choir. I will protect Angadha. Do not worry about him. While they were speaking, Vali closed his eyes and slept permanently. Angadha came and broke into tears at his father's body.

Later Hanuman preached Vedantha to Tara who is the wife of Vali. Tara told that she would follow her husband. She later killed herself, unable to bear her husband's death. With much grief all of them cremated their bodies according to traditions.

After that Rama and others went to Sugreeva who was in grief and consoled him. Hanuman and other Vanaras saluted Rama with respect for getting back their kingdom which had been in hands of Vali over the years. Rama ordered them to make Angadha as their prince. They then requested him come into their kingdom but Rama rejected their proposal as he was in the forest exile for fourteen years. In a few more my exile will be completed.

Rama continued, "In the month of Karthika, you should help me in killing Ravana. Meanwhile you enter your kingdom and rule it, leading your life luxuriously. This is our united promise. Stand on it"

Later Sugreeva entered his kingdom with his vanaras. And they did his coronation as a king and Angadha as their prince. Ruma, Sugreeva's wife, became the queen of Kishkinda.

After Sugreeva had been crowned, Rama and Laxmana decided to stay in the same cave in Rishyamukha hill where Sugreeva and his army lived. After going into the cave, Rama spoke with Laxmana in this way, "This cave is so wide and well ventilated. We should stay here until the monsoon completes. The place is nice to live in but I am more worried about Sita. That night Rama couldn't sleep as Sita's memories were haunting him. Laxmana tried to console him but it went in vain. They both thought about how they would know about Ravana. How they would get back Sita. Laxmana said that Sugreeva would try to find Ravana meanwhile we would be very patient for four months.

Sugreeva on the other hand was enjoying his life in the kingdom. He was on a different pilgrimage with his wife. He handed over all his duties to his ministers. And Hanuman especially was taking care of everything. He and his people were on cloud nine.

Hanuman said, "We are happy because of Rama. We should not forget his help. So it is our duty to search for Sita. We have about one crore of soldiers. We should send them in different directions to search for her. Our four months came to an end in three days. If we don't search, we will be given death punishment by Rama"

So Hanuman ordered his soldiers to go and search for her

all over the world.

Sugreeva went to Neeludu who had one crore soldiers. He wanted to take his help in identifying Sita. Neela and his soldiers started searching for Sita.

Rama on the other hand felt dejected. He felt four months to be four years. Laxmana found his desperation in his brother. He also could do nothing but to console him. Then Rama told his brother, "Sugreeva forgot his duty. He took my help but forgot to help me. So you go to Sugreeva's kingdom and order him to be very angry with him.

Laxmana went to Kishkinda and met Sugreeva. He had shown very much anger on Sugreeva. With his red face, he warned Sugreeva and asked him if he wanted to be killed as his brother by Rama. He asked him why he had forgotten his task. Even Angadhà also told his uncle that Rama was angry with him. But Sugreeva did not respond to them. Then the vanaras came and played the music. With that music he came out of the sleep. Then he came to know that Laxmana had come to meet him and they also told that Rama was very angry at him for neglecting.

Sugreeva then understood Laxmana's rage after he was told by Angadha and the ministers. He was surprised why Laxmana was angry with him. He didn't understand what mistake had been made by him. Then Hanuman recalled his promise to Rama. He said that he had completely forgotten searching for Sita. The given time was over but we didn't try for it. Rama was also angry with him as he had made a mistake. Go and ask apology to Laxmana otherwise we will be killed.

Meanwhile Laxmana entered the room where Sugreeva was

resting. He was terrified of Laxmana. Tara and Ruma came to Sugreeva's rescue. They pleaded with Laxmana to appease them. Then Laxmana remembered his task. Then Sugreeva said that he had started searching for Sita. He said that he had sent Neela's army for the task.

Sugreeva apologized to Laxmana. On knowing the truth, Laxmana was appeased. Then Sugreeva became free from fear. He said that he had gotten his kingdom due to Rama. How he would forget his duty so simply. I would only help him in identifying Ravana's place. Rama himself has to kill Ravana and get back Sita. Sugreeva repented for his mistake and said sorry.

Then Laxmana told, "You know Rama is a man of righteousness. I am unable to console him being a brother. He was gloomy with the loss of his wife. So let's do something for him"

Sugreeva ordered Hanuman to bring all of his army to the kingdom. Within ten days we should try to find Sita. We have an army of crores. Everyone should perform their duty. It is his order otherwise death punishment will be imposed for those who neglect his duty. Hanuman immediately went and told the news to all the vanaras. They all rushed to the kingdom and stood before Sugreeva. Sugreeva felt very happy. They came with several gifts but he rejected all of them. He told them that they needed Sita's appearance. They immediately went searching for Sita.

Sugreeva later went with Laxmana to meet Rama. On seeing Rama, he fell on his feet, asking for an apology. Rama felt very happy on seeing his army who came to search for his wife. Then Rama embraced Sugreeva with a friendly gesture. Rama said that the time for war is approaching. Sugreeva told Rama that his men would go and get Sita back after killing Ravana. Rama felt very happy with the words of Sugreeva.

Rama thanked Sugreeva for helping him in identifying Sita. He said, "It's like the sun has risen in my life. I am very fortunate to have you as my friend. I will conquer anyone if you stand by my side. Ravana abducted Sita for his downfall. I will kill him with my sharp arrows soon" Meanwhile crores of vanaras came and stood before Sugreeva. They were waiting for his order.

Sugreeva said to Rama, "With your permission, I will send vanaras for the task" Rama replied that as it was his army, he told Sugreeva to order them. He said that he wanted to know Sita soon. Firstly Sugreeva sent one lakh vanaras to the east in search of Sita. He gave them a month's time. If they don't come in time, they will be given death penalty.

Later he sent Neeludu, Hanuman, Jamba antha and others to the south. The team was headed by Angadha. And he sent his uncle and others to the west.

Sugreeva at last sent Shatha Bali and the team to the North. He ordered them to search for her in every nook and corner of the world. After a few days the teams from the west and north came and said that they had not found Sita anywhere. And the team from the east told the same. So they came to the conclusion that Sita had been taken south. So it was possible for Hanuman to take her back.

Hanuman and the other vanaras went in the direction of the south but they didn't find Sita anywhere. They didn't stop searching for her. They were eating fruits and stems and proceeding further. They even went into the deepest part of the forest where there were no animals. There they found Kandu Maharshi, who had a lot of anger. Since Maharshi lost his son who was just ten years old, he cursed the forest.

The vanaras team went into the cave but they did not see Sita there. They saw a raakshasa which was like a big hill. He saw the vanaras and tried to attack them. Then Angadha beat him with his palm, with which the raakshasa fell onto the ground, vomiting the blood. They found another cave and they also went into the cave. Even there, they didn't see Sita.

The vanaras spoke to each other, "We searched for Sita everywhere but we couldn't find her. At least we could not find the evidence. If we don't find, Sugreeva will punish us so let's not dejected. We should have persistence now"

Then Angadha and the team went south again. They saw many hills but no use. They took a rest under the trees and proceeded. They reached the mountain of Vindhya. They searched all the caves of the mountain. Hanuman searched for her at every nook and corner.

There they found a cave which was guarded by a raakshasa. They saw the swans and other birds were coming out as there were plenty of fruits and flowers. They were coming out for their food. The vanaras were astonished to see a lady who wore fabric clothes. Hanuman went to her and asked who she was.

Hanuman went to the lady and asked in this way, "We are exhausted and feel very thirsty. Whose is this golden tree? How beautiful the flowers are! How the golden tortoises are roaming!"

Then the lady replied to Hanuman, "Here a sacred man lives here. He built this golden forest. His name is Mayavi. He had performed the great penance for that Lord Brahma appeared and gave him a boon. He lived happily for some years. Lord Indra told to kill him for showing his lust on Hema, who was a damsel. Later Indra gave this to Hema. I was born in Merusavarni. My name is Swayamprabha. Now I am looking after it" She asked Hanuman how they had come here. Before answering to her, she told them to have fruits and water.

Then all the vanaras had the fruits and water. Then their exhaust had disappeared. Hanuman started narrating their story. He told what had happened to Rama from Ayodhya episode to Sugreeva's episode. He told her that they had come here with the order of their king, Sugreeva. Then Swayamprabha was very happy with them. Hanuman requested her to save them as the given time by Sugreeva was over. So they requested her to send them back. Then Swayamprabha told them to close their eyes and they did so. She strictly told them not to open their eyes. When they closed their eyes, to their astonishment, they came out within a minute.

After Swayamprabha had gone, Vanaras crossed the forest and there they found a sea. It was roaring and rising with its waves. When they went there, Sugreeva's time with Sugreeva was over. They felt very sad for not fulfilling their king's desire.

Angadha told the vanaras that they couldn't fulfil their task so it was better to die rather than going back. They decided to kill themselves. But vanaras were afraid of Angadha's idea. But they knew that their king would kill them if they went without telling Sita's news.

Tarudu was one of the vanaras told that they would live in the cave. Here plenty of fruits and stems are available. If we live here, no one could harm them. The other vanaras appreciated his idea.

Then Angadha started crying for his position. Then all the vanaras told that this was because of Sugreeva. He unnecessarily had given this task to us. They started praising Vali and cursing Sugreeva for keeping them in this position. When they were worrying, they suddenly heard a strange voice from the cave.

All the vanaras decided to kill themselves. Just then an eagle appeared before them. Its name was Sampathi, who was the younger brother of Jatayu. It came from the cave. Seeing them, it asked vanaras, who were in grief. Then Hanuman told Sampathi, "We have come here in search of Sita. Our king, Sugreeva, sent us to find her. We did not fulfil, given task. Rama was worrying about Sita for his wife's abduction. Jatayu also tried to save her but Ravana killed it. As we didn't succeed, we are killing ourselves"

Then Sampathi got angry as Jatayu was its brother. It asked, "Who was that cruel fellow? How dare he kill my brother? It asked them all the details how and why had happened all the incident"

It said that its wings had been burnt due to the sun's shine. So it was unable to fly and hid itself in the cave. Then

Angadha went and took it down from the hill. He started narrating the whole story of Rama and Sita. Why they had been exiled. How Rama had killed the rakshasas. How Maricha disguised as the golden deer. How Jatayu tried to help Sita while Ravana was taking it away. He told her that Sita had dropped her jewels as evidence for Rama.

Then Sampathi said that Ravana was the brother of Kubera. He lives in Lanka. When they asked about Lankha's address, it said that it was very far away. You have to cross the big sea. The sea was spread about 1500 kilometers. If you cross it, you will find Lankha. There Sita was imprisoned in the garden of Ashoka. The rakshasas were guarding her. You can see Ravana also there. The vanaras were stupefied with the reply of Sampathi.

Sampathi asked them to take it near to the sea so that they could do its brother's rituals. They did so and it performed the rituals to its brother, Jatayu. At last vanaras felt very happy for knowing the secret of Sita. Sampathi also told them that its son, Suparswa had seen Ravana's abduction.

The vanaras discussed themselves that the news made them happy but who would cross the sea which was very broader and longer in size. They knew nobody could cross it and come back. They asked Jambavantha for advice. Then Jambavantha told not to worry. He said that Hanuman could do the task easily. Jambavantha started telling the greatness of Hanuman. He opined that Hanuman had all the qualities. He was equal to Rama, Laxmana and Sugreeva. Apart from the physical strength, Hanuman was mentally strong.

Jambavantha started narrating Hanuman's childhood story. He was the son of the wind god. He told the adventures Hanuman had done during his childhood. Finally Jambavantha came to the conclusion that Hanuman was the only person to fly and cross the sea. All the vanaras started motivating Hanuman to fly. They clapped and praised to fly.

Hanuman then knew his power and at once he rose very big in size. His body expanded to a hundred times bigger than the previous. He said, "I am the son of the wind god. I can cross the sea with my strength. I can break the earth and lift the hill. Suddenly he rose to the sky and the vanaras felt as if they were looking Vamana"

Hanuman then flew at the speed of wind. Within seconds he was in the sky and moving above the sky. All the vanaras were dumbfounded. The vanaras left their grief and were surprised. They did not think that Hanuman could cross the sea. They bid him the grand farewell, telling that their lives would depend on him.

Hanuman started his journey in the sky like an airplane. He crossed the mountain of Mahendra. When he stepped on the hill, it roared with a big voice. The animals on it were afraid of the sound. From there he started his journey to Lankha.